# Spirits of the Dead

Thy soul shall find itself alone
'Mid dark thoughts of the grey tomb-stone
Not one, of all the crowd, to pry
Into thine hour of secrecy.

Be silent in that solitude
Which is not loneliness – for then
The spirits of the dead, who stood
In life before thee, are again
In death around thee, and their will
Shall overshadow thee; be still

The night, though clear, shall frown
And the starts shall not look down
From their high thrones in the Heaven
With light like hopes to mortals given,
But their red orbs, without beam,
To thy weariness shall seem
As a burning and a fever
Which would cling to thee forever.

Now are thoughts thou shalt not banish,
Now are visions ne'er to vanish;
From thy spirit shall they pass
No more, like dew-drop from the grass,

The breeze, the breath of God, is still,
And the mist upon the hill
Shadowy, shadowy, yet unbroken
Is a symbol and a token,
How it hangs upon the trees,
A mystery of mysteries!

~ Edgar Allan Poe

*Shadow of the Ghost Hunter: Seeking the Paranormal Truth*

# Shadow

# of the

# Ghost Hunter

## Seeking the Paranormal Truth

*To Ed + Valerie,*
*Happy Hunting!*
*Dan LaFave*

## Dan LaFave

**Edited by Connie LaFave**

# Table of Contents

# Foreword – Author's Note

The preternatural or paranormal world consists of that certain pseudoscience which appears outside or beyond the means of modern everyday natural science as the average person understands it. Upon seeing this term, a person will ask what pseudoscience is and what does it actually mean or characterize. The definition of pseudoscience as to the American Heritage Dictionary is any theory, methodology, or practice that is considered to be without scientific foundation. This simply means more directly that this is an area of research as a science or practice that has not readily been accepted yet within the normal confines of the scientific community as being confirmed proven fact or reality because of the lack of any scientific evidence foundation. An example of some other practices out there like this might be considered acupuncture, herbal medicine, or possibly even spiritual healing in a sense. Many people see the natural world around us as just being what our eyes and senses perceive that everyday modern science has proven or created around us.

Within this natural scientific world, there are many gray, dark areas that exist which are not readily understandable to the average person except for what we have been taught in school as to the accepted scientific methods and modern science. Even though we cannot always see or sense electricity, magnetic fields, microwave fields, or even nuclear energy, we all are born into this world and shown that certain scientific methods, electricity and other forms of energy and evidence, do exist and are proven without any doubt or disbelief. While some of these other existing gray areas in modern day science may include what is more commonly referred by many as the realm of the supernatural, the preternatural or paranormal may also include any strange event or an extra-ordinary phenomenon that occurs and is characterized as being 'beyond' the capacity of common understanding in the natural scientific theory world.

Many people at one time or another have had some type of unexplained and what we call "supernatural event" happen during the course of our lifetimes that we cannot readily explain through modern scientific methods and reasoning. When these unexplained events do happen, many of us may try to keep it to ourselves because of how strange the event was, or we may choose to share the experience with others. One of the most difficult things for us in the acceptance of these unexplained events as possibly being supernatural in nature, are our own personal single attempts at trying to believe if the strange events actually occurred or if they were just our imagination.

Many of us from the time when we were young children to now, may have had these strange unexplainable events occur which scared or terrified us to some degree. We may have tried to get help or reasoning at the time from older people only to be told that it was all just our imagination and that we were just making it all up. These strange events may have led so many of us as children in being afraid of the darkness and what may lurk unseen and stalking within that darkness. Society may have somehow indoctrinated or imposed a certain mental material thinking as to these things being explained as being simply make-believe in nature and fictitious. Perhaps these unexplained events that so many of us have had at one time or another are what lead us as young children in describing the well-known myths and legends that we all know of as to the boogey man and many other imaginary dark creatures that are described in our many famous fairy tales, myths, and folklore.

A person has to take the time to really sit back and wonder why and where many of the myths, stories, urban legends, or fairy tales originated in our culture and why. Many of the fairy tales and myths seem to have originated from within the dark and not openly talked about places that dwell right within the existence of our lives and society. Children and adults question if these strange experiences that have occurred are real or maybe preternatural or paranormal in nature. We ask ourselves if these strange experiences we have had border on being labeled supernatural; the answer to that question is quite clear, precise, and simple – the answer is yes!!!

Many people may still not want to accept the paranormal pseudo-science reality that ghosts and hauntings might definitely exist in the natural scientific world we live in. During many years of doing paranormal research, helping many common everyday normal very rational people, I have realized and can confirm without a doubt to the fact that ghosts and hauntings as a strange enigma do exist in our world. How they exist is another question. Ghosts and hauntings are a true every day reality for many very credible and logical people out there, and there are very strange unknown things beyond our senses and way of normal conformed thinking which do actually go bump in the night.

There are many reasons why I felt I needed to write this particular book as to my sole contribution to the whole paranormal research investigative field in general. I have seen that the interest in ghosts and the possibility that they do exist is becoming increasingly higher each and every year. A person can guess that on this specific question out there, they will discover that surprisingly, about 70% of the general public does now believe in the possible existence of ghosts and hauntings. I have seen more and more people coming out of their shells over the last decade and admitting that they have had at least one phenomenal supernatural event in their lives which astonished them and for which they never had any natural explanation for. I have also found in deep discussion that many people will not talk openly about this subject unless another person starts the conversation on what they have witnessed or encountered before.

There are also many people who generalize the whole paranormal investigative field as being taboo, or in their own words, a certain 'hogwash' mentality. There are many skeptics and extreme haters to this field of paranormal research who quite readily and strongly dispute this field and all the very reliable and compelling every day evidence that is presented from this field of research in general. Many critics exist in this field that will say that it is all simply make believe, pure sensationalism, or that the people experiencing these strange supernatural events in their lives are developing a certain mental condition or illness.

There are also fakes, cons, frauds, and manipulators out there who unfortunately hurt the good of the whole paranormal research field as to what it is really trying to provide, deep, lifelong answers, that many people seek as to what actually becomes of us and our families when we die and leave this physical material world of existence as we know it. The question that I have been asked many times as a paranormal investigator is if there is an existence or real heavenly place for us after we die and leave our physical bodies. I must say that I personally believe the skeptics to this field do not really think about this big question until when they themselves are about to die and see the true reality.

There was one solitary reason in all of my thoughts that stood out, however, as to the true reason I needed to make all of the pertinent information that I know available. I once had a good friend who was relatively new to this research field in discussion specifically ask me one night if I had a book, from my vast library of many paranormal authors, that he could borrow that would help him get a better overall learning and understanding of this research field and that would talk about all the ins and outs of paranormal investigative research and why things are done one way versus another way by everyone who is involved in this research field. I thought that I had a book like this in my paranormal research library, which contains many other very well-known names and authorities in the paranormal field that I could let him borrow to read that would answer all of his various questions he was directing towards me. He had a lot of questions for me that night.

You see, one who is experienced can easily discuss the paranormal investigative research field all night for several hours with a person who is curious and still not be able or even close to covering everything in total detail. Upon examining and reviewing my entire library collection of paranormal investigative books that I have acquired over the years, I soon realized that I did not have one sole book that truly answered all the questions he was directing towards me that night. I found upon examination, that most of the very well written books that I have on the paranormal field of ghosts, only really talk about individual investigative cases and experiences that other investigators have had over the years and their thoughts and conclusions on those investigations, but no real in depth down to earth paranormal investigative research knowledge or analysis of why things are done a certain way versus another in this field.

Everyone hears ghost stories all the time, but people don't really get the answers they need or are seeking from these types of stories. I then realized that I must sit down and write this book so that people like my friend new to this research field and any other ordinary people with an interest towards ghosts and hauntings could have some kind of well-rounded understanding and knowledge in the beginning as to everything that is involved in conducting good proper paranormal investigation.

I also wanted to provide some very good available information on this particular field of research without a person having to acquire and read all sorts of books on the subject. I look to share my experience and knowledge with any new and also those already experienced investigators whom are seeking answers to their questions. I do feel and hope that all my past experience and information in this book will help the general public and anyone interested in becoming a good paranormal investigator. I hope that this book helps the general public and other investigators already in this field learn and study everything they can about the paranormal research field and the true nature of ghosts and hauntings collectively. I also hope that everyone will learn from the internal politics that seem to strongly emanate from and within this field of research.

The paranormal investigative research field is and always will be a constant learning environment for everyone involved within it, and we should all have fun in exploration and learning as much that this intriguing research field can provide to us. All investigators, whether new or already in this field, should strive to conserve what this research field is about, band together to help each other through networking to learn more, and bring this field of research to the very helm of modern everyday science as to acceptance and understanding. This book is dedicated to my wife and soul partner, Connie LaFave, who also is the co-founder and another good lead investigator of our organization, Graveyard Shift Paranormal Investigations, who has stood by my side through thick and thin and who greatly inspired me as a professional paranormal investigator to share all my thoughts and experiences with the public in writing this book.

Dan LaFave

# Prologue

The night so far in the house had been quiet. Quiet, that is compared to what would usually occur sometimes during the many paranormal investigations I had conducted in the past. Now, several hours into this one particular investigation, I was beginning to think the rest of the night was going to be quiet also. The paranormal investigative team this night consisted of five people, including myself, as well as the elderly client, her daughter, and her granddaughter. This was a very normal looking modern house by perspective. Not the usual stereotypical, spooky old house one might think of as having paranormal occurrences happening or being deemed haunted in nature. This was a rather newer house that not even the neighbors who were very close by would have ever suspected as being possibly haunted. This one night was very dark for some reason, not the usual night darkness that I was accustomed to during the investigations of the past. This might have been for the fact that there was no moon at all on this one particular night.

This elderly client had lost her loving husband only a few years ago. I could easily see that she was missing him a lot in how she talked about him and how she presented herself with all her mannerisms. In observing her, she seemed very lonely to me, but at the same time, she had a very good clear rational mind for her age and was independent. I thought to myself that this person was extremely interesting in how she described her and her husband's marriage and long life together. They had done a lot together during their lives and all that time they had been together. They seemed like they were a very happy couple and were married for many years. They had a very long lasting loving relationship. Her husband had passed away a few years before from a very sudden heart attack that was unexpected.

After her husband's passing, the client had described her house as being very lonely and quiet. Nothing out of the ordinary in the house had ever occurred until almost a year before this investigation. Then a series of very strange occurrences and events started to happen within the house on a daily basis that was unnerving the client and her daughter to quite some extent.

She had described the first event a year ago as being one that seemed somewhat normal, but also very strange at the same time. She had been watching television alone in the house one night and heard the doorbell go off like it had gone off so many times before when people had came calling for some reason during the day. She had stated that it was about eight pm and dark outside. This time however, when the doorbell went off, she had thought to herself that maybe it was a neighbor, since it was getting late and too late really for a sales person to be at the door.

She got up out of her recliner which was not easy due to her age and slowly walked to the door. She had a front door that had two opaque glass panels on either side of the door where you could see the outline of a person standing outside as you approached the door. She had her porchlight on and she could easily see the outlined dark shape and shadow of a tall person standing there and swaying slightly from side to side outside as she walked up to the front door. The figure appeared to be male due to its size and shape. The doorbell even rang again as she was walking up to the door to open it. She then looked again at the swaying shape standing outside and turned the doorknob slowly, opened the door, and to her surprise there was no one standing outside on her porch. After a moment, she opened the screen door and walked out onto her porch and then onto her front sidewalk thinking the person had started to walk away. She walked out onto her driveway and looked all directions and could see no one outside. Even though she thought this to be very strange, she just assumed that somehow the person who had rung her doorbell had just walked away.

This particular event and many other strange disturbing unexplainable events over the course of a year were described when the client's daughter called requesting that an investigation be conducted to see what was occurring to her mother and what was actually happening in her mother's house. Her daughter had described strange activity that included levitating religious objects that floated across the room and then dropped, objects disappearing into thin air from where they were placed previously and then reappearing in same place or other place in house, religious artifacts falling mysteriously off of shelves and breaking, strange, strong, constantly changing odors like rotting flesh and cigar smoke, moving shadows, and a very dark ominous male shaped spooky apparition seen within the house by her mother on more than one occasion. All of this scared her mother so badly, that her mother not only locked her bedroom door at night from the rest of the house, but also put garden tools and other things to block and hold the door. Her daughter and the client wanted to make sure that they were not losing their minds in all of this because they had both individually and together witnessed and experienced many things over the course of a few months that really seemed strange and unnatural. The client literally wanted to make sure due to her age, that she was not losing her mind in all of this and her daughter was worrying the same in that she felt her mother maybe could not live alone anymore.

In all the years of conducting investigations and interviewing clients, I had seen this perception many times before from people. I would talk with people on cases who were very professional and normal people in their daily work lives, but who on the other hand thought they were going crazy in what they were experiencing in their personal lives. The events that this client and her daughter had witnessed and observed seemed to fit this particular scenario of very rational people having very strange and scary events occurring to them. The events described to me and the teams by this client were very frequent in nature in that they would occur on a daily or weekly basis. This alarmed me greatly and I knew that I personally had to do what I could to get to the bottom of what was happening to this client. The fact that she was very elderly also put an extreme urgency on the case because I did not want this client to have to suffer as to her health.

After setting up all of our equipment in the client's house which consisted of placing 2 or 3 video infra-red mini-digital video (dv) camcorders on tripods, electro-magnetic field meters, infra-red motion detectors, digital and analog voice recorders, non-contact infrared thermometers, and a KII EMF meter, myself and the rest of the team had started this paranormal investigation at 10 pm sharp. I and teams I have been associated with before in the past would on occasion use what is a called a DVR (Digital Video Recorder) monitor camera video system for larger location investigations to help cover more area, but due to the size of this clients home being smaller, the DVR system was not needed or available that night. I, as a lead investigator, would usually set the time parameters of any paranormal investigation for at least five hours in a client's home or location. It would have been longer by a few hours if our team detected paranormal activity occurring in some way. We had the clients sitting very quietly in the living room area with all of our investigators during the course of the investigation that night.

For this investigation, we had the whole house completely dark. We needed to have it very dark because our infra-red camcorders could see in the dark and better detect strange paranormal anomalies

14

on video for any possible evidence. This night again was very dark, and I had a hard time just seeing my hand in front of my face and trying to not trip over things walking around in the dark. It makes it very hard for investigators to move around because we always do our investigations in complete darkness. It is very easy to bump into something, knock something over, or fall and hurt ourselves. Since I was a very experienced investigator and had been doing investigations now for several years in conditions such as this, I was very accustomed to walking around in the complete dark by myself without any problems at all. My eyes always have adjusted to the dark very well. I have always told people that I think I see better in the dark at times than in the light because of doing so many investigations in total darkness.

Many people would always ask me if I was scared to walk by myself in the dark, and I would just laugh and tell them that I could actually see better in the darkness than in the daylight and that I was perfectly fine going off to investigate things on my own. The time was approximately 12:30 A.M. and nothing really out of the ordinary had occurred that particular night except for a few cold spots and personal feelings of being watched like other times felt by the clients and a few of the other investigators. I was beginning to think that nothing of any real substance was going to happen.

I had earlier in the night set up an infra-red mini-dv camcorder on a tripod recording in the back client's master bedroom which also had a bathroom joining it. I had also set one of my infra-red motion detectors on a nightstand at the foot of the client's bed that stood approximately three and a half feet. On top of this nightstand table was also a small television. My infra-red motion detector had a series of 3 blinking lights on it. A green light which means that it was not active, a yellow light which means that it has been activated and would go active in two minutes, giving an investigator enough time to get out of the area, and a red light which means that it is activated and covering an area. The motion detector would emit eight infra-red beams out of it at different angles. If something moved in a location and broke or disturbed one of those beams somehow, then the motion detector would go off a few seconds later sensing the movement.

I had been turning this motion detector off and on throughout the night when either myself or other investigators went back to investigate that particular room or area. I had however activated the motion detector about thirty minutes earlier with nothing happening, because we were all doing some EVP (Electronic Voice Phenomena) sessions in the living room which means that we were recording and asking questions to see if we could capture any disembodied voices or noises on the recordings to our questions. It had been very quiet throughout the night and while we were doing these EVP recording sessions.

I was the closest person standing directly by the hallway leaning on the wall. Suddenly, during one of the other investigator questions, my motion detector went off very loudly with an ear piercing scream in the other room. This startled everyone in the house because of the loud siren sound it was emitting. I immediately turned and ran down the hallway to see what it was, thinking that maybe it had just accidently gone off somehow. When I opened the door to slowly walk in and peer in around the corner towards where the motion detector was, I could see the blinking red light going off repeatedly as the loud screaming sound was exploding my eardrums. For a second, I did not think anything of this as I was about to turn my motion detector off with the hand held remote switch I had. It was then that I really looked at the situation unfolding in front of my eyes and quickly noticed something that made my hair stand up. Again, I had initially placed my meter on the nightstand which was approximately three and a half feet off the floor next to the television set. The television set sat up another two feet or so on the nightstand.

My blinking motion detector was now hovering approximately two feet above the television just floating in mid-air. It was a motion detector that also could be plugged into the wall and I had plugged it in earlier into the wall between the nightstand and the client's bed to help conserve on its individual battery power source. In this second of amazement towards my motion detector floating in mid-air, I failed to see the real reason behind this phenomenon happening. As I stood there, briefly with my eyes adjusting more to the extreme darkness, to my horror I could see there was a very dark black mass shape of a male looking figure standing right next to the meter appearing to hold the meter. This shape had no distinguishing features about it except that it looked like a male figure and that it was very tall like a man and was cloaked as if wearing a hood. The black mass figure also was much darker than the other darkness around it to where it was very visible to the naked eye against the background of the darkness. It suddenly whirled around towards me as to look and threw the meter down so hard that I could hear the meter crash on the floor and see the power cord come flying out of the plug on the wall. The black dark entity then twisted around completely away from me in a flash and darted at an unearthly speed between the client's bed and wall directly into another nightstand next to the bed and directly though the wall towards the outside area between the houses.

This scene before my own eyes completely startled and astonished me as an investigator. Even though I had been doing professional paranormal investigation for a few years now up to this point and had experienced all types of paranormal confirmed activity occurring up to this time, I had never witnessed something quite as extraordinary as this. The other investigators had come down the hallway quickly behind me asking what had happened and I could not verbally speak about what I had actually witnessed for a few minutes because of my shock on how this particular situation just occurred and what I had just seen. I had suddenly remembered then that there was a video camcorder in the room on the tripod and it was aimed directly in the direction of what I had just seen. I thought to myself that I must have the best evidence on video that any investigator could ever hope for in this business.

It was then that I discovered upon inspecting it, that my video camcorder had somehow been turned off mysteriously, several minutes of this event occurring even though no one had been in the room and I had made sure that the video camcorder had been actively recording with plenty of video tape when I left the room and closed the door. It had over an hours recording time left on it, but the video camera had turned off approximately five minutes of this event occurring. Did that dark shape mass somehow turn my camera off? Did it somehow have intelligence to know how to do all of this? Did I actually startle this thing when I walked into the room? Was this black dark shape figured mass in the process of inspecting my motion detector to see what it was after it went off? Did I somehow surprise this unknown entity as it was roaming around in this client's bedroom?

These were all questions that suddenly were going off like fireworks in my head. I was trying to rationalize what I had just seen and experienced as a very seasoned paranormal investigator. The fact is that I had just seen something that brings many other investigators in a sincere passion to this field on a daily basis and why the paranormal field has grown to such high levels of exposure in the last few years. That something that drives us as ordinary people from many various other professional career fields of work to want to do professional paranormal investigation as a second very important demanding weekend research study career for the rest of our lives.

Research is something that makes us all question the reality around us and helps bring us that much closer to the true religious and scientific belief that there is really some other existence out there for sure past our death of the human body, and our mental consciousness. The main question however to me as a lead investigator at that point and many other countless investigators in this field was how I would present this experience, and any other possible captured paranormal evidence to the rest of the general and scientific world in such a fashion that it would be believed by other people out there and not be ridiculed as to being a research field that consists of being labeled pure taboo by its skeptics.

# Chapter 1: Paranormal Investigation Curiosity

When I now, as a professional paranormal investigator, meet people at any meeting, lecture, or public/private presentation that I do, the question of how did I really get interested in this field of research will usually always come up as one of the first questions. As to answering this question, it is always somewhat easy for me to answer because I simply look back on the many years that I have done paranormal investigation research and what my first great experience was to make me really want to become a professional investigator and give me the driving passion and dedication to want to do this unselfishly forevermore as a life-long study. What really brought me to the paranormal research field was one of my several extreme haunting experiences several years ago that I had never been able to forget...

I had acquired and read information from several paranormal books about good haunted hotels generally across the whole United States and Texas. I had specifically read one book that described many different haunted hotels, bed and breakfasts, etc. in Texas where a person could find such a haunted location. I also had heard much about the very haunted Myrtles Plantation in St. Francisville, Louisiana, where one could always possibly experience something there. The problem for me at the time was the distance and cost factor involved. St. Francisville, Louisiana would be at least a nine hour drive for me where as many so-called haunted hotels listed in this particular book were a much closer drive in my home state of Texas. I then decided to do extensive research on the internet as to trying to find a very good haunted hotel to stay in because I wanted to have a true haunted experience that would be remembered.

As I perused this book, there was one chapter which really caught my eye that described Jefferson, Texas as having a very haunted history and being possibly one of the most haunted towns per its population and size within the United States. Specifically it named several locations within small Jefferson, Texas that were rumored to be very haunted and the Jefferson Hotel was right at the top of that list. I had never been to Jefferson, Texas and it was much closer than St. Francisville, Louisiana to me, so I decided at that time that this would be the place I would visit as to my quest.

When I first got to Jefferson, Texas and the Jefferson Hotel, I could easily see why so many people were fascinated by the history of this old city. The city dated back to the early 1800's during the days when steamboat travel was very popular and were the major means of travel besides the railroad, horseback, and wagon. As I and my companion walked into the main parlor reception area of the hotel, we were very impressed by the old, historic allure that the room presented to me. I felt like I had stepped back in time for a moment. The cobble-stone streets and many of the historic old buildings in the town were the same way. Even though I had never been to this historical, beautiful city before, I felt for some reason, a past attachment to the place. I walked up to the front desk to check in and pay for my three day stay in Jefferson, Texas at the Jefferson Hotel.

During all of the research I had done, I had read many haunted tales from past guests who had stayed at the Jefferson Hotel. The tales were very interesting and some were very scary to say the least. This is what brought me to the hotel because these many strange accounts were from very ordinary people just like me. I remember asking the desk clerk if she knew some of the stories and she told me of some very good ones that she knew. She also told me at the time that the hotel did not really want to attract people solely because of its haunted nature, but rather for the historic beauty of the hotel and city. I perfectly understood what she was stating. She went on to tell me about all sorts of recent activity in certain rooms of the hotel. I soon learned that approximately half of the 24 rooms in the hotel had reported haunted paranormal activity recently. I have to admit that I was a little bit skeptical then, and initially thought that these might just be stories to try to lure the public to the hotel as a way of making profit.

After I got the room key and all of our bags, the desk clerk instructed me on where Room 6 was upstairs. Once I arrived in the room and unpacked, I then sat on the edge of the bed and found myself constantly expecting something to happen at any moment. It is funny when a person thinks about it. One cannot imagine the feeling a person has the first time they are staying in a hotel room or hotel that is very rumored to be haunted. Even though the rooms look like very average hotel rooms, they suddenly take on a mysterious mystique. A person finds themselves constantly looking behind and jumping at every single noise in the room, thing happened until approximately 11:30 P.M. that first night in room 6. I was lying in bed watching the television which was on a cabinet at the end of the bed towards my feet.

My companion had fallen asleep and she was a very sound sleeper.....the dead could not even wake her because of the medications she was taking at the time. I was lying on the top of the covers in my shorts and a t-shirt wondering if I would experience anything in this room tonight and of course what would happen the moment I fell asleep. My arms were exposed at the time and I had my right arm resting on my right leg which was slightly hanging off the bed. I was lying on the side of the bed closest to the lone window and wall. There was just enough space on that side of the bed for a person to walk. Suddenly, I started to feel an electrical sensation around the tips of my fingers on my right hand. The sensation then quickly took shape to me as to that of a small woman's or girl's hand. The invisible hand motion then began to slightly stroke and rubs the hairs on my right arm. I just lay there shocked staring in disbelief at my hand and what was occurring at that moment. I had a hard time believing what I was feeling. I then felt the hand and fingers actually start to drag up my arm as if someone was walking up the side of the bed draping their fingers on my arm. I felt a slight movement of very cold air on that side of my body and had the sensation that something or someone had just walked past me and was now standing in the corner between the bed and wall staring at me.

The temperature on that side of my body between the bed and wall was also dropping quite considerably and was very cold and uncomfortable, like a freezer. I then, after a few seconds, could not take it anymore and I jumped out of bed and stood there in disbelief, astonished that something unseen and invisible to the naked eye had just touched me. My companion woke up and I explained my story, but of course she did not believe me. I also had the strongest feeling now that whatever it was had moved to the corner of the room and was just staring at me. Then the feeling and experience was gone as quickly as it had appeared. Nothing else happened to me that night, but I did not sleep very soundly because of the previous experience and the high anxiety and anticipation level that was created as a result of it. I literally jumped at the sound of every noise in the hallway or the room that night.

The next morning we moved across the hallway into room 12 which was quite a bit larger and decorated better than room 6. This room had a large antique looking king size posted bed in it and seemed much more grand and historic looking than Room 6.

After my experience the night before, I was wondering what other surprises awaited me in this new room. I got unpacked and settled in that day with nothing else out of the ordinary happening. It was when we had gotten ready to go to dinner that I noticed something very strange. I had a pair of black dress shoes that I had put in no particular order by the side of the bed earlier that day. When I looked, I could now see that both shoes were sitting upright on their heels next to each other against the wall near the closet. Something had positioned my shoes so that I would notice them. I was very surprised and laughed about that experience. Nothing else happened till late that night around 1:00 A.M. I had grown bored and ventured into the upstairs hallway and sat in an antique couch that is positioned at the end of the hallway next to the locked balcony door. My companion had stayed in the room sleeping or something.

This door had a glass section in the upper part of the door from which you could watch the street in front of the hotel. The hotel was working on fixing up the outside second floor balcony at the time and there was no way to get onto the balcony short of going through that locked door. It was approximately 1:30 A.M. when I started to experience things in the hallway. There were no other guests up and about except for myself and it was very quiet inside the hotel and outside on the street in front of the hotel. It was then that I started to hear the strange noises. I kept hearing things moving down the upstairs hallway and would look up suddenly and see nothing. The hotel had an old historic typewriter sitting on a table halfway down the hallway. These strange movement noises seemed to come from this typewriter area but I could see no one. It also sounded like someone would hit a key to the typewriter every once in a while to get my attention. These were not your average simple noises either. It was like a person or persons were moving about in the hallway. I could hear what sounded like a few footsteps every ten minutes or so. I would hear something move just about every time I looked down. When I looked back up, the noises would stop completely, but then I would have the strong feelings that I was being watched by something or someone down that hallway. I also turned a few times to look outside and saw that there was no activity outside. I had heard a loud noise at one point and turned and looked down the hallway once again to see what had made the sound.

It was when I did this that three very loud knocks came directly onto the glass behind me on the locked balcony door. This startled me greatly and I literally pounced like a cat about three or four feet off the chair I was sitting on. Once I managed to catch my breath, I then turned and walked back up to the door and looked out onto the balcony. There was nothing out there at all and no one on the street at that late hour. It was a very quiet and eerie feeling. I still had the distinct feeling of being watched by some unseen presence that was playing games with my mind, but from where I could not tell exactly. I then gathered myself and decided to go head back to my room and go to bed. Nothing else happened that night.

The next morning we got ready to move into the infamous much rumored by people to be haunted room 19. I had walked down the hallway to speak to one of the maids to ask her if the room was ready for me to move my bags and clothing. She said that it was okay and told me the story of room 19 and if we were ready to spend a night in there. She also then proceeded to tell me what happened late to the guest the night before that stayed in room 19 before me. The main story concerning room 19 was that a prostitute long ago had been either stabbed or strangled by someone and left to die in the bathtub. The maid also said that sometimes her ghost will actually turn the faucets off and on and you could actually hear this through the closed bathroom door. A person staying in the room can turn on both the sink and bathtub hot water faucets and then turn off the lights and close the door. This is when you can hear someone turning the water off and on. When a person goes back into the bathroom after several minutes, you are supposed to be able to see the words "Help Me" written in the mirror in the steam condensation on the mirror.

She said that a lot of very strange things happen to people in room 19, and that some people will simply leave in the middle of the night. The woman guest in room 19 the night before had done this exact same thing. The housekeeper told me that the guest had left that morning around 4:30 A.M. and would not even go back to her room for her bags. The hotel staff and her other personal friends had to get her stuff and remove it for her. While the maid was telling me this story of what happened, the woman's personal lady friend came out of another room across the hall from room 19. During her story, she went on to tell me that they had decided to do a Ouija board session in room 19 the night before to see what might happen. The woman who was staying in the room had been laying on the bed watching her two other friends as they were sitting on the floor doing the Ouija session.

They had apparently asked the board several questions and dared something to happen to them. They had also asked if a past attempted murder had taken place in the room and if anyone had died from that. The board answered yes to these questions and they then asked the board who had actually died in the room. The board then answered the name Laura. It was at that moment that some invisible force came up behind the woman on the bed and grabbed her legs pushing her down against the bed and holding her. The unseen force held her for several seconds in which she could not move at all. It then had released its grip and she screamed and jumped off the bed. This really scared the woman and it appears that several other unknown things happened to her while in that room causing her to go down to the lobby in the middle of the night and leave the hotel.

This really surprised me hearing this news of what happened. I was beginning to wonder if staying in room 19 was a good idea after all these things happening the night before. We also were going to be the only guests staying in the hotel that night. When we got into the room, I could hardly wait to try the bathroom trick I had heard about from the maid. I turned the tub and sink hot water on just like I had been told. I then turned off the bathroom light and closed the door. I could hear the water running and I waited approximately five minutes before opening the bathroom door again. Before I had started the trick, I examined the mirror very carefully and there was nothing that I could see or feel on it as to any film or words. When I opened the door, the words "Help Me" appeared in the mirror. The words were written very funny and were not even at all. It was if someone who was in distress had written them.

We carefully examined the mirror over and over again looking for any signs of foul play or trickery. I noticed that there was a certain kind of film on the mirror that these words consisted of. I scratched the film with my fingernails to the extent that the words and film were all smeared up all over the mirror and the words were unreadable. I then did the same test again and closed the door. When I opened up the door, I again was shocked. The words appeared exactly as they had the first time with no smearing or scratching at all in the mirror. I ran the test several times and never heard the faucets turn off. It was on the fourth attempt that I saw something that really intrigued me. This time my first name appeared under the other words in the mirror. I decided at that time to quit doing the experiments because it was really starting to bother and scare me.

It dawned on me again that we would be alone in the hotel this night. I got the idea that it would be really neat if the desk clerk could possibly unlock all the upstairs rooms for us so that I could investigate all the upstairs rooms if I encountered or heard anything during the night. The desk clerk was very receptive and positive to this and she proceeded to come upstairs and unlock the doors for me. She thought that it was very exciting as to what I wanted to do. She had told me a story of a previous desk clerk who had quit. He was working late one night when a thunder storm was coming in. There was no one staying in the hotel due to being a slow weeknight. He was checking the hotel on his final rounds upstairs. As he proceeded to check and lock up each upstairs room coming from the backside, he saw that suddenly all the doors started to slam open and close on their own, the upstairs lights started flickering off and on, and very strange noises occurred.

Apparently he ran downstairs to call the owners that he was leaving the hotel to come give them the keys, was quitting, and not coming back again. This story only added more mystery as to what I was intending to do that night as to investigating. I assured her that I would not touch anything in the rooms that I just wanted to have access in case I heard or encountered anything. We then went around town a little bit and later went to bed to catch some sleep for our late night adventure. At around 1:00 A.M., we decided to leave the room door open and ventured out into the upstairs hallway midway and sat on different antique couches there across and down the hallway. It was very quiet and spooky in the hotel at that time because we were alone, or so we thought. The lights were on in the hallway, but the hotel hallway still presented a spooky image that late at night. Even though we existed in the present, the mood of the hotel suddenly presented and took on an image of being very rustic and old, as if we were living in the past. A person would feel that they have stepped through a portal back in time to the 1800's or something. The upstairs doors were all unlocked but closed.

I had first decided to venture into the haunted room 14 which was right down the hallway. This room had a queen size bed with an old carved heavy ornate headboard that went almost to the ceiling. This bed was not any ordinary bed in description. I had never before seen a bed with a headboard as high as this one. The story I had heard of this particular room was that a woman had become distressed in the past and somehow hung herself from the top of that headboard. Her fiancée had suddenly upon their wedding day told her that he did not want to marry her. She then supposedly became very emotional and suicidal, and supposedly hung herself from the top of that headboard. There was a big crack at the top of the headboard from what I could see, and the story there was that it could not fully support her body weight and this caused the headboard to crack slightly.

I could see upon close visual examination that the big tall headboard actually could and would be strong enough to hold a person if attempts on their life like this was made. I initially had thought this was just a story to scare the guests and make them nervous. The hotel had purchased this bed sometime ago and had put the bed in room 12 for several years without anything happening. The hotel then decided to move the bed from room 12 next door to room 14. That was when they claim a lot of strange activity reportedly started happening in room 14 to guests staying in the room. I walked in without turning on the light and closed the door. I proceeded to sit on the bed and faced the door to see if I could be a witness to anything in this room. The hallway light was coming under the door, and that gave me just enough light for my eyes to adjust to the darkness around me. The room was very cold and much colder than the other rooms I had checked out that night. The room, after a few minutes, seemed to take on a very eerie cold feeling that seemed extremely abnormal.

It gave me goose bumps from the coldness that did not feel right to me at all. I had a feeling like I was not alone in this room and had this feeling again for most of the night up to this point. I sat on the bed for about three to five minutes staring around the very dark room with nothing happening, when all of a sudden I felt a strong force pushing up under the mattress right under me. It was strong enough to lift my body up and down on the mattress. I experienced this for approximately eight seconds before I decided to jump off of the bed. When I turned and looked back at the bed, it appeared that something was lying on the bed indenting the mattress and that the mattress was breathing in a strange fashion from between the mattress and box spring. I could still see the mattress going up and down slightly as if in a regular inhaling and exhaling breathing motion. I could not believe what my eyes were seeing. This caused me to go back out into the hallway in disbelief at what I had just encountered. I got my companion and brought her in explaining, but by then the strange event had stopped.

It made me question the reality of what I had just seen. Did I really see and feel what thought I had just experienced? I stood in the hallway at great disbelief as to what had just occurred. How could something get under that mattress and lift my whole entire 6'-4", 265 pound frame up and down. It felt just like a person lifting me up from under that mattress. Even though I tried to find ways to discredit what had just happened to me, I knew in my own mind that it really did occur and that I was not losing my mind in imagining that very strange paranormal event.

Nothing else happened that night and we decided to go to bed because I knew I had to make the road trip back home in the morning. I got up early the next morning and decided to rest a little while in the rocking chair that was in my room. My companion again was sleeping like a zombie in the bed under the influence of her medications. I had the hotel journal of ghostly experiences that guests write about on during their stays in all the rooms examine. The desk clerk had given this to me the first night, but I had forgotten to read the guest accounts up till now. I started to read all the past guest accounts which were very good, but I also then decided for old time's sake to do the bathroom trick one more time. I expected that same thing to happen as all the other times. I went in the bathroom and turned the hot water on again in both the tub and sink. I then turned out the light and closed the bathroom door. I proceeded to sit back in the rocking chair and start reading the journal again.

Approximately 30 seconds to a minute later, I distinctly heard both faucets turn themselves off and the water stop. I knew this because I had turned the hot water on high on both faucets and the flowing water was very loud in the room even from behind the closed door. I could hear the loud squeaking sound that the faucets made as they were turned off by someone or something in the bathroom. The moment that the water stopped running and I could hear water droplets falling in the bathtub, I heard a faint woman's voice saying "Oh" over and over. It sounded to me like that was the word distinctly, but I may have been wrong. Maybe it was "No". It was really scary as I listened to it, and I was very surprised and frozen because here it was happening in the morning during daylight hours. It sounded like a faint broken record repeating itself over and over again slowly and then speeding up. I was sitting there trying to decide from where in the room I was hearing this strange sounding voice. It definitely was female. I even called to my companion quietly to try to make her wake up to hear what I was hearing, but she again was like a dead person in the bed. I finally decided that the voice appeared to be coming from behind the window shade. It was sunny out that Monday morning, but I had drawn the window shade all the way down making the room rather dark and gloomy. No sunlight entered the room from that one lone window.

I got up and walked over to the window to investigate what the voice sound was. I then could hear that the noise was actually getting louder the closer I got to the window. As I got closer to the window, the noise became more distinct. I could tell for sure that it was saying "Oh" or "No" and that it was a woman who sounded like she was in severe pain and duress. As I reached and pulled the shade back slightly, the sun's rays began to enter the room. It was at that moment that the woman's voice stopped abruptly and the water faucets both turned back on at the same time in the bathroom. The water sound began again as the water flowed. I then turned and ran into the bathroom, but there was nothing unusual in the bathroom. There was no writing on the mirror like last time. This time there was not even any steam in the bathroom even though I could see steam rising up from all the collected water in the bathtub and sink. I did manage at that point to wake up my companion somehow and explained to her what had just occurred, but it did not seem to affect her thinking due to her not experiencing what I had witnessed. Shortly after this event however, both myself and my companion did witness the big light fixture above us start to spin and sway on its own as it someone was doing that, it also did this upon us asking the woman spirit in name to do something to convince us she was there.

I was definitely convinced during my stay that there were very strange unseen things going bump in the night at the Jefferson Hotel located in Jefferson, Texas. As to what exactly was causing these strange events to happen was an entirely different story and explanation and needed a whole lot more review and investigation. As I thought more about what had occurred to me those three days, I realized that I had gotten exactly what I had been looking for as to my quest.

This was to spend the night in a very haunted hotel and walk away with a certain everlasting memory that would always be there for me. I must admit that a lot of it did unnerve me slightly because I was unseasoned in those days as to being a good paranormal investigator. It was these strange paranormal events and many others before and after that created the strong passion for me wanting to become a professional paranormal investigator and learn more as to researching ghosts and hauntings. I had to, in my own personal quest; determine how and why ghosts and hauntings occurred to people. From that moment forward, I had the deep passion and drive required to make this an ongoing lifetime study as to providing possible answers and theories as to what may be occurring. I wanted to divide what could be naturally occurring versus what may be paranormal or haunting in nature. I also pledged from that moment on that I as a professional paranormal investigator would do my best to help any people out there encountering strange, scary events such as these.

From what I have seen, paranormal events like these are usually what draw most people to the paranormal and the possible existence of ghosts. People want to explore and confirm more as to what they personally have witnessed. These people are not strange for wanting to do this; they are just looking for answers to their many questions on the very strange paranormal events they are encountering in their lives. This is what honestly and sincerely draws people to want to do paranormal investigation, that deep strong passion and desire to seek more answers and learn about ghosts and why they are here

# Chapter 2: Is Paranormal Investigation for Everyone?

I wanted to state a few things here about how easy and exciting it is for anyone and everyone to investigate the paranormal research field and explore ghosts and hauntings. It does not take a fancy degree or certification from a university, institution, or any organization for a person to do this. As to any organization offering a special certification, I found that being a professional paranormal investigator that is best to steer clear of any places such as these that charge a fee for a certification. Giving a course or certification in this field is fine by me, but it is unethical to charge people for it unless you absolutely have to because of needed expenses and resources. It is just ridiculous to think that a person would have to pay money to want to do paranormal investigation and study ghosts and hauntings. Having something written on paper does not make a person a good paranormal investigator. Doing this the right way just takes some proper know how, advice, where to start, and of course some experience doing it. Is paranormal investigation for everyone? The answer to this question could go both ways and could be debatable.

One might think there is a lot involved for any person to start, but the reality is that it is actually very easy and does not cost a lot of money for the initial equipment needed. The number one thing a person needs to ask themselves however is why does he or she want to do this? What exactly are you trying to accomplish by exploring this field as a paranormal investigator and what are you hoping to get out of this? Do you want to do this because of the numbers of exciting paranormal shows now on television, or do you have a personal sincere passion to go about this on a much lower scale by yourself with a lot of time and dedication? Do you want to investigate ghost and hauntings just for the sake of being a thrill seeker as to all the shows you have seen on television? Do you just want simply to see a true ghost for yourself? Are you just looking for a lot of excitement because you are bored with your life?

The reasons I state this are quite simple. I have met many people over the years and had many discussions over this topic and question. Many people that I have talked or interviewed within the past who want to become paranormal investigators have given reasons which are usually all the same. Most people have told me that they wanted to do this now simply because of the fact that they saw this on television and that it looked exciting and that they were just looking for something else to do in their lives because they were bored. I usually start off these conversations by telling and advising these people looking for a scare thrill that they are just wasting their time doing this and that they do not really know the true involvement of passion, hard work, dedication, and the time that is required in doing good paranormal investigation. I know this may sound blunt like a baseball bat hitting your head, but it is the truth.

Now, I do not want to give the impression here that I am trying to turn good people away from this research field. This is not my true purpose at all in telling and being blunt about this. I am always one for more people coming on board this research field, even though this is happening in droves now because of the vast popularity that the media has brought to this field within the last few years. I remember once several years back when you typed in the word "paranormal investigation" on the internet and this only returned back a few hits as to organizations out there. Now when a person types this in, there are thousands of hits that come up. I am simply trying to relate information to people out there who tell me that they just want to do this because of what they saw on television or read about in the newspaper. An example of this is how much attention the paranormal investigation field has gotten lately in just the last ten year period. Most of this attention has really garnered over the last five years or so.

This is because of the numerous television shows out there that depict professional paranormal investigation and what we as investigators to this field do and possibly find during our investigations. Most people will watch any thirty minute to an hour long show of a paranormal team at a certain rumored haunted location and see all sorts of things happen during the course of the one episode. Well, the reality is that sure, a paranormal team might be encountering certain exciting paranormal things on that show, but the public does not realize the amount of work, time, and editing necessary for that paranormal team to accomplish its mission in getting this evidence and presenting it on television. There are usually very long tedious hours when nothing is occurring during an investigation and then there of course are the many other long hours that are needed as to analyzing all the audio and video that was acquired during the investigation.

I have been a past team manager and lead investigator with a very well-known and established TAPS (The Atlantic Paranormal Society) family member investigative team out of San Antonio, and also a past lead investigator with other established paranormal teams in San Antonio, and now also the present founder/lead investigator of my own paranormal investigation organization, *Graveyard Shift Paranormal Investigations* (*GSPI*), which is located in Harlingen, Texas. I feel that from all my past experience that I can now speak in a good perspective light in my observations from the many years doing this what is truly involved in conducting paranormal investigations well and right each and every time. There are many levels to paranormal investigative work, and a person needs to ask themselves in the beginning exactly what it is that he or she is seeking.

Are you just wanting to do this on a very casual basis or are you wanting to be in a professional team environment doing things on a much grander and organized scale, helping clients/people in extreme need of assistance? A person also needs to ask what brings them to this field and what they hope to get out of it in the end. A person also needs to ask themselves if they can really handle this field as a serious and overly demanding second job and research study all the time using management and dedication. I say this because I have known so many people in the past that told me they were there to help the team and its clients no matter what, 120% of the time only to fizzle out and completely disappear as an investigator three to four months later after only a handful of investigative cases and literally no help from them looking for and setting up cases. Many of these people also seemed upon initial interviewing like they might turn out to be very decent investigators in the end. The reasons for this usual disappearance or lack of following through demise are very clear and I will talk about these more in detail.

On the levels of paranormal investigation, many people out there simply want to associate in so-called paranormal social groups to discuss hunting ghosts in general, their past haunting experiences, or maybe just go on one or two paranormal investigations at most to see what it is really like doing this. I have heard many of these types of people tell me that they only wanted to have the chance and thrill to see an actual true ghost and have a haunting experience. That is fine by me to have these types of people because they are at least being honest and up front on what they are truly looking for. I will usually kindly direct these types of people to any social ghost hunting amateur groups in the area. It is the other percentage of people that I usually see a problem occur. This is to say that I always get along very nicely and respectfully with mostly every person I meet or with whom I associate. What I am really talking about here are the people that I take a lot of my time to interview very carefully who want to join a professional paranormal investigation team. There are always going to be team guidelines and parameters that a person must strictly adhere and follow. Of these, client confidentiality is of the upmost importance. As a professional paranormal investigator, we serve the clients who come to us who need help and needing answers. As a team in this environment, we must represent an image to the clients who seek us out that is professional, sincere, honest, respectful, and experienced.

One might think this to be easy, but clearly is not. Once a professional paranormal team is created for a purpose and mission, there should be main preset management guidelines and responsibilities just like any business or corporation out there. A team is just this, everyone on the team must act as one for the overall good of this research field and all the clients that are served or helped by that particular team. When one looks at any real professional paranormal investigative team, you will clearly see a well-defined internal management structure if that team is on the highest possible level as it should be when it comes to doing investigations, giving public or private presentations, or helping its clients or the public community in any manner. It is so easy for any team out there to call themselves true professionals when in fact they are not or do not act professional in the sense of the word. This is why it is so important that every investigator on that team be acting on their upmost highest integrity level and accordance to the team mission, rules and guidelines, and organizational structure that have already been determined by management.

When a person decides that they want to investigate on a higher level and want to join a team somewhere, the first step is always for that person to contact a paranormal investigation team in some fashion. This is usually through the internet, phone, media, or so forth. There are many very good teams out there to join, but I have to admit that there are also many bad ones. It is not always easy finding the right team and fit. An easy way of doing this is to first do extensive research of teams you may find on the internet or elsewhere. See what things these teams have done and how long these teams have been around. Are these teams all about haunted promotion to just make money or are they really more about researching this field and helping people? Do some of these teams really try to glorify things with the wording on their websites? You have to be careful about things like that when looking around. There is a big difference between a paranormal team that is sincere in what they do and one that is simply out there to make money strictly through promotion. There are teams that may take donations and this is okay because this field of research can become very expensive over time as to any travel and equipment expenses.

Once you have done this research on your own and have narrowed down a list of potential teams, the next step is by contacting the teams to see if they have any open positions or slots as we call them that need to be filled. If they do have actual open positions for new investigators, they will tell you or not through either a phone interview, email, or in person if you have the individual characteristics or experience that they are looking for. It is just like any job out there when it comes to the interviewing process to see if a person is the right fit for the organization and if the organization is the right fit for that person. A business would not be hiring someone without an engineering background or credentials if they were seeking or needing a position that needed an actual engineer with that training and expertise. Please do not be let down if many teams in the beginning turn you down the first go around or other times after that. This is very likely to happen to you on the first run since you really are just a novice and unknown to this research field.

Please do not give up hope if this happens to you. One thing that I have seen many people do however is get very angry when these rejections happen and start comparing their other day-time job qualifications to what the paranormal teams are looking for as to positions. There are many very good paranormal investigators in this field and many of us are professionals in many other highly respected fields as well. Being a lawyer, doctor, psychologist, nurse, professor, etc. however does not guarantee that a person will make a good investigator for any particular team. I have in the past had people on levels like this really argue and tell me that I was making a very bad choice in not selecting them and that I would be sorry. It was like they were threatening the paranormal organization just because they were not getting picked for the position. They would not take no for an answer.

I found that people like this only came off as sounding far too important and did not seem like they would take orders well or be a good fit within a team system. I even had a board certified medical psychologist contact me once who expressed sincere and genuine interest as to wanting to become a paranormal investigator and learn this field. After many telephone calls and emails, we finally found and made the time to meet with this psychologist in person. He was interviewed by me and other people in the paranormal organization and then left afterwards. After speaking amongst ourselves for about thirty minutes if he was the right fit or not for the position, we all mutually agreed that it would be very good to have his expertise on the team and that we would all show him the ropes as to learning good paranormal investigation on the team. When I later contacted him by phone, I left several voicemails for him which were not answered or returned. I then sent several emails advising him that we had agreed that he would be good for the team and that we were all welcoming him on board. Still no responses at all from this psychologist and he simply disappeared. This kind of thing actually happened quite frequently with people and it was very frustrating because these people wasted a lot of our time and energy only to show disinterest later. Again, I want to emphasize that having a fancy degree in some other professional field is not an automatic qualification as to becoming a really good paranormal investigator and finding out everything that could be learned of this research field from people with many years experience doing it.

I have seen many people who get angry about rejection in the beginning go off and try to form their very own paranormal investigative team quickly and then try to bad mouth all the paranormal teams that rejected them before. This is fine and okay because we do live in a free country that allows this and everyone has their own right to try something new, but one must realize that this will not solve anything and it just creates bad feelings because of the lack of experience that most people have in this field. It also is not moral or respective. The ill spoken part towards other teams in the field also is very unrespectable and shows the true unprofessional character of an everyday want-to-be paranormal team. Other teams learn about this because word of mouth does travel quite often more than you think in this field and people learn who the very good reputable paranormal investigative teams are and who the very bad, unethical, and untrusting teams are.

Nearly 60 to 70 % of the teams formed quickly in this negative manner usually most likely fail and disappear in the first six months to a year of their existence. This is because once these teams are formed and they look for places to investigate, they then find out that they are not very well-known at all as to getting actual cases and just are another ordinary paranormal team on the block without any experience doing this. They are not able to get cases or even case-referrals for this sole reason and everyone soon becomes very bored with the whole concept. It is often at this time that the internal team bickering begins because of extreme impatience of the team members, and the whole team soon disbands in under a year or so. Teams like this usually also end up breaking many rules and laws in general. These types of teams usually end up running around private cemeteries, abandoned scary looking buildings, or homes at night looking for any paranormal happenings to investigate. This is all very illegal, very dangerous on liability to say the least, and also very unprofessional as to the paranormal research field. Many people can get seriously hurt doing this as they stomp around abandoned buildings that are in need of repair. What teams that do this kind of thing must realize is that someone out there does own these properties in some capacity even if the properties are not well kept or falling apart.

I do not want people to feel upon reviewing my thoughts and past experiences in seeing this kind of thing that it is not impossible to start and have your own very successful paranormal investigative organization. It is always possible if every person and team member in a reputable paranormal investigative organization follows the main rules of establishment and guidance towards doing paranormal investigation in general. The main rules as I have seen, come up with, and devised over the years are as follows:

1) Always first create your organization legal client investigative liability and consent documents that your clients acknowledge and sign, establish your team mission and by-laws as to how your organization will be run as to how investigations are conducted, and also state clearly what the exact organization rules are that need to be followed by each individual team

43

member per the organization and all investigations that are done. Then have each team member acknowledge and sign your rules or by-laws as to being a part of the organization. Even if you are already friends or relatives with each member, this still needs to be done from a legal organization viewpoint to ensure that everything is always followed accordingly. Establish a certain probation period for each new team member and make sure they understand what is required and what actions can constitute them being let go from the team if the rules are not followed accordingly.

2) Determine in the beginning who the leaders are and how the management of the organization will be followed and observed by each team member. Establish titles for each team member as they come into the organization and make sure that every team member follows a certain chain of command as to any questions they have or if any on the job training or discipline is needed or warranted. Always be respectful as to the main management of any organization and also towards your individual members. Proper respect warrants respect if it is given right each and every time by each team organization member.

3) It also is not good to have too large of an investigative team unless this is specifically needed as to heavy client caseload. It is normally recommended to have no larger than six team members when any paranormal organization is first started. Having too many investigators in any one place during an investigation can cause problems on that investigation and the organization as a whole. It is generally best to probably have no more than four or five investigators present for any one investigation unless the premises are large and more investigators are needed. You always want to have one or two investigators who are considered just backup in case someone assigned for a particular investigation gets suddenly ill or has some

other emergency occur where they cannot be at a client's scheduled investigation. You need to have back-ups because you never really want to cancel out on investigations for your clients. Your clients have taken a lot of time to make their home or business available to your team for that investigation and it is not fair and unprofessional to put any clients in those positions. As a new team gets and does more client investigative cases, then it normally is a good rule to cycle all your investigators in and out to get them the proper training and guidance that they need as to learning to become a good paranormal investigator.

4) As to starting any paranormal investigative organization, it is always good to get all your proper training and experience first as a leader before you begin teaching other new team members around you. This may sound very simple and straightforward, but you need to remember that if you have not done paranormal investigation for very long with actual client cases under your belt, then how do you expect to properly train the other new investigative team members that have joined your team. It takes time to learn, and then train other people. Being an eager beaver and getting out there too quickly can only mean disaster in this field. In other words, don't just get a group of people together who state that they like to hunt ghosts and just go out there trying to do this. You will fail in the worst ways if the proper steps are not taken.

This field is all about learning each and every day, but you must first have a certain level of experience towards this field before you can properly lead any investigative team. Most teams find this out the hard way the very first time they do a scheduled client case. They think they have what it takes and then show up at a clients home or business. That client is watching everything the team initially first says and does. If a team has no organization whatsoever in it, a client will easily see this in the beginning. If that paranormal investigative team just appears to be a bunch of inexperienced thrill seekers, then anyone out there will see that and your over all reputation will go down the drain before you have managed to even accomplish anything. It is easy to say that you want and will go out to acquire evidence of ghosts and hauntings by means of investigation, but a team can easily become sloppy as to their organization and technique. This is the difference between what a very professional paranormal organization is and what the very unprofessional organizations are. The professional organizations end up creating a very reputable name for themselves doing correct protocol method paranormal investigation for say ten, twenty, or thirty years at least and the unprofessional organizations are gone and disappear in as little as a year.

5) Networking in this field with other reputable paranormal organizations is also the key to getting your name, experience, and investigative methods known out there. There are so many paranormal investigative organizations out there that are very selfish and want to take and eat all the apples in this field and any clients in general. These types of teams always give the cold shoulder to other teams that have been out there for quite some time doing this already. This could mean that another team might contact you get some needed assistance with a project, lecture presentation, or any other special event that might come up in your area. A lot of teams out there will give the cold shoulder in these situations when contacted because they do not want to have to share the spotlight with any other paranormal organization. This is because they are only concerned about what they do and how their name is known in this field. The truth of the matter is that if any new paranormal organization adopts a principle such as this, then that organization's name will in reality become mud in the paranormal networking community.

You may not know it, but other paranormal organizations will know who you are and that you are not to be trusted and that you are not genuine as to networking and helping others in this field. Any very successful paranormal organization out there is always open to networking and helping any other paranormal organizations in any way needed. It also helps with any client case referrals. If another organization cannot do a certain client case for any reason, then they might refer it to your paranormal organization because they will remember how you helped them before and this serves as your means of being trusted and reputable. You also must have a very open mind to constantly listening and learning other methods if you ever work as an organization with anyone else. If you do not, then you will come across as to being simply arrogant and this again will hurt your reputation in the long run.

6) Proper client case management is also very important in this field. If any organization is disorganized in any manner with its leadership and how they do things, then that organization will usually turn out to have very sloppy time management and case file management for all its clients. This means that things will not be followed accordingly again the same way each time for any particular case that comes your way or things will simply become lost later if needed as to evidence, so forth. Things as to the case and possible evidence will usually end up getting lost or misplaced and then forgotten about. There is a right and wrong way to doing proper case management. I of course am going to do my best at trying to point out the right ways versus the wrong ways here because I have learned from experience all of the right and wrong pros and cons as to doing this.

I learned in the beginning that I was doing several things wrong. I was listening to someone in this field several years ago who only wanted investigations done his way as to his organization methods and would not budge on anyone else's suggestions. He always did every investigation the way that he wanted and he kept all the investigative case information to himself for the sole purpose of profiting from it all and making himself sound better than others. I am not saying that he was doing all of his investigations incorrectly, but I did have very mixed feelings about the ways he was conducting his investigations and the so-called evidence he said that he acquired from the investigations. I had respect for this investigator as to his ideas, but internally I did not agree on how he did his investigations and I had a professional difference of opinion. Then, after leaving that organization, I later learned from other very good investigators in this field and managed to 'tweak' a lot of how I did my investigations and my methods.

When you first get contacted by a potential client by email, phone, or other means, it is always important to get as much information as possible from that client in the beginning. Create an interview form where you always ask the same direct questions of the client. Draft up an initial copy of questions you want to ask each time and then put all those questions into your format. Get used to asking these same questions over the phone to your clients initially so that they do not get the idea that you don't know what you are doing.

Create a good flow and conversation with the client to make them feel more comfortable and also so that you can better analyze what they are telling you. Make sure that you write very fast on all of your notes on the questions being asked. You need all of this information initially to determine if that case is even worthwhile as to your team doing an investigation. You don't want to waste your team's energy and time and you also don't want to waste a client's time if there is a strong chance you might not be able to get any possible evidence. You need to ask yourself upon acquiring information from the client if there is even a chance that your team could help them as to acquiring any possible evidence. This is always done by an initial phone interview in the beginning once you receive some form of communication from a potential client. You always get all the who, what, when, where, why, and how as to any possible activity during the initial client interview. You need to determine how often things occur and what types of things occur that are witnessed or felt by the client.

If there is not a high frequency of unexplained things occurring to any particular client during a recent time period, then it is feasible that the case is not worth taking. This is because you as a team will not be in that client's home or business for very long and the chances of getting any evidence are going to be very slim. Remember that all of the clients live in their homes 24/7 possibly experiencing things whereas your team would only be there for a few hours conducting an investigation. You must also establish per that initial phone interview on what the client's mental status is. Do they appear rational or irrational as to what they are telling you? Do they appear credible? Have the clients themselves tried to rule out all possible natural causes as to personally investigating? Why do they need your help and why should an investigation be done? What do they want to find out exactly? Are they just contacting you for the thrill of having a paranormal investigative team in their home or business for publicity? Are they going to freak out if your team does find something as to paranormal evidence occurring in their home or business? How might they handle your team observations?

These are all questions we must ask as investigators in the beginning as to any potential client cases. Any possible paranormal evidence must also be documented very carefully and all team member investigator analysis must be done on the same levels and protocol for each individual case to ensure that all possible evidence is acquired the right way and that it is protected for further analysis, review, and professional opinion by everyone on the team and also your clients. It is always also very important to protect your client's confidentiality as to their information being kept private and sealed if that client requests this. As to any evidence, you also must make sure that you can possibly acquire and use this for paranormal research by your team and this field in general. In other words, make sure you have clients sign and acknowledge that you can reserve use of any possible paranormal evidence acquired for your own means, but that you will protect the client's identities and location and keep this information hidden from public view and observation. You will find that many clients will most certainly agree to this and it is important because you as an investigator can then present any possible evidence you or your team acquires to the public and paranormal world for review.

The last thing any investigator wants to do is acquire something very important as to paranormal evidence, and then not be able to present that evidence because the proper protocol of getting permission from the client was not followed. A client could always possibly state that they do not give you permission to use the evidence after the investigation is already completed if you do not first have that permission in writing. Always sit down with your client before the investigation takes place and fully explain all of the legal ramifications concerning liability, release, consent, and how the investigation will be conducted on their property. In this research field, this process is what always separates the good professional paranormal teams from the very bad teams out there. Every new paranormal investigator to this field has to ask himself or herself in the beginning what kind of investigator they want to be.

# Chapter 3: Being Prepared with the Proper Equipment

I do remember a time in the beginning when I only had one piece of equipment for paranormal investigation. I also remember a time many years ago when I first really had an interest in the paranormal research field and was wondering on how to go about it all and get started out there. I was very happy with my one piece of paranormal equipment, but at the same time wondered how I was going to get anything with it. My desire at being a paranormal researcher went back to when I was a child because of my large interest in ghosts and hauntings, but I never really knew how to go about it all as to conducting the research. I was reading books about ghosts and hauntings at a very young age. My mother saw this interest early on and used to buy me what are now considered to be paranormal books. I used to read a lot of ghost stories about people's real life experiences and used to think to myself that there has to be a better way of confirming those haunted events that people have. I used to see in most ghost stories that these people appeared to not have any help in understanding what was occurring to them. It seemed that most ghost stories were only out there to scare people and did not provide the scientific explanation side necessary as to what really was occurring with these haunting events the people in these stories were encountering.

When I later in life decided to start my study into paranormal investigation, I soon found this was not easy by any means in the beginning several years ago. I did not know who exactly to personally ask when I started out in this field. When I began, paranormal investigation was not as widely known as it is now because of more television and radio media. Most paranormal investigation books in bookstores were all stuck away in a hidden corner section that was hard to find. I always had to ask the bookstore personnel where to find the books I was seeking and they would sometimes look at me strange when I asked as if I was a satanic worshiper or something. A lot has changed since when I first started doing this. There were not that many paranormal investigation teams or organizations out there to contact. I had to do a lot of research and study of other known reputable paranormal groups and investigators out there in existence already, buy a lot of paranormal research books that were available in reading up on everything I could, and determine what steps I would take in starting out as a serious paranormal investigator on my own.

One of the first obstacles I had was what equipment to buy and the cost of that equipment in getting started. This is something every new paranormal investigator will encounter. I soon realized that a person could go broke pretty quickly if it was not done the right way in acquiring equipment. I was not rich and most true good researchers in this field are not rich because we offer all our investigative services totally free to our clients and anyone in need of assistance. True paranormal researchers do not charge a cent for any services that we provide. We are always available for help to anyone in need and do not charge anything for our services which include investigations or consultations. It is very easy for any new paranormal investigator to say that I will go right out and buy everything that is needed to conduct a good solid paranormal investigation. The truth of the matter is that this can easily run someone several thousand dollars to do this and most of us simply do not have that kind of the money in the beginning to run out and buy everything that is needed as to having standard paranormal investigative equipment. Also, if your spouse, boyfriend, or girlfriend is not really into you doing this kind of thing, spending that kind of big money could develop into a lot of arguments and possibly a relationship problem or split later. My wife and I have acquired the equipment that we have presently over a ten year period and we from time to time add another piece of paranormal equipment to our assortment of equipment that we already use.

In asking yourself what essential items any good paranormal investigator should have in conducting an investigation the right way, I would recommend a few items in the beginning that are a necessity so that you can properly get good evidence for analysis. I would recommend that you buy an audio digital audio recorder or an analog recorder (a person can get something like this at just about any electronics store out there for a very decent affordable price), a good digital and 35 mm camera (any brand will do here and a digital camera better because of the cost of the film/developing for the 35 mm camera), a handheld camcorder with infrared technology built into it (a word of advice here , there is only one name brand, SONY, period out there currently with this technology in their camcorders), an individual infrared light to mount on your camcorder, an EMF (electro-magnetic field) meter, and an infrared non-contact thermometer (to register temperature changes throughout an environment without you having to change position). Any person with access to the internet can type the key words in doing an internet search for these paranormal items and get all sorts of hits in looking for the right purchase price.

The reality is that a person is not going to be able to afford all of this in one shopping spree unless you are rich, so I would suggest that a person view this suggested paranormal equipment list first and determine what aspect of paranormal investigative research field they would like to explore first – the audio or the visual. It does not matter what piece of equipment you buy first to use in your investigations, but it does matter that you do good research and know how to use that equipment you buy the right way in getting the proper results you are looking for. I have always told my associate investigators in the beginning that they should know everything there is to know everything about using the equipment they buy first before moving on to other pieces of equipment. I have also told my own investigative team members that they should have the required equipment in being able to conduct a scheduled investigation even if one or two members cannot be there at the investigation for some reason. In other words, the client in need of the investigation should never suffer an investigation having to be cancelled last minute just because one or two investigators cannot be there for some reason unexpectedly. The scheduled investigation must always go on unless dire consequences present themselves to the situation.

I want to next explain the essential paranormal investigative items analog or digital audio recorder, digital or 35 mm camera, SONY camcorder with infrared technology with accompanying individual infrared light, EMF meter, and infrared non-contact thermometer and how and why these items are used and why they are essential for any good paranormal investigator to have. As I said before, if you want to take your experience in the paranormal investigative research field to the next level as to this being more than just a hobby or interest, it would be essential for you as an investigator at some time to have each one of the items I mentioned previously as to your basic equipment. I have seen many new paranormal investigators start off with only a digital audio recorder or possibly just a digital camera, and that is okay because I suggested and have seen that these items are expensive and it does take time to get everything.

What I and many other experienced investigators out there do not like to see, however is an investigator that has been on a team for quite some time that still only has the same items that they initially started off with. In other words, they still only have that one camera or digital audio recorder they started with years back. Any person wanting to be a good investigator in this field is only shooting themselves in the foot so to speak in doing this, because your passion in doing this is not really shining through and you are just wasting yours or others' time. Every good solid reputable investigator whose name is known out there has made many large sacrifices in getting to the place that they are currently in the paranormal investigative community. This includes a lot of expense, dedication, and devotion over a very long period of time in getting to where he or she is. If a person still only has that one digital camera or one digital audio recorder that is used during investigations after say a one year period, then that person simply is not in this field for the right reasons. There is strong reason to believe in this scenario that a person such as this is probably just tagging along with a paranormal investigative team for the thrill of possibly seeing a ghost or experiencing something paranormal.

When it comes to the many paranormal investigative cases I have conducted myself or been a member of, I have always taken a direct interest as to audio aspects of paranormal research when it comes to ghosts and hauntings. This is because of the many EVP's (Electronic Voice Phenomenon) recordings I have obtained over the years doing this. I have gathered EVP recordings from all sorts of places. One would think that you can only gather an EVP recording late at night from some dark spooky old house, cemetery, or abandoned building that society and time has forgotten about. This is quite the contrary as to the many EVP ghostly recordings I have obtained over the years.

Many EVP's I have gotten are from very ordinary places and I also have acquired them in direct sunlight on very beautiful days. I have managed to gather EVP recordings from business establishments, new modern houses that everyday people live in, parks, historic buildings, hotels, cemeteries, and so forth. My wife and I have even managed to capture what we consider to be authentic EVP woman speaking recordings right from within our own house under very controlled recording sessions that only the two of us conducted. This may sound strange to some people, but you would be surprised to learn how easy it is to use audio recording means to capture EVP's. I will talk and discuss more about EVP's (Electronic Voice Phenomenon), and what they possibly are, and why paranormal researchers consider them important, in a later chapter.

When it comes to capturing good EVP's, a good investigator again must be using either a digital or analog audio recorder. Most paranormal researchers in the field today use digital audio recorders. This is because digital recorders are much easier to monitor and use for proper analysis on computers as to the sound analyzing software programs that are out there. It is also believed by myself and many other reputable paranormal researchers in this field that the white noise (the electrical noise for which the intensity or range is the same at all frequencies within a given certain band) generated by digital audio recorders makes for better, clearer, and louder EVP recordings. This is not to say that a good researcher can use the good old fashioned analog tape recorder because recorders like this have also produced good results for many researchers. Many investigators new to this field in the beginning will wonder what digital recorders are best to buy and this field has always suggested either Olympus, Sony, RCA, to name a few brands that will work. My wife uses a RCA recorder that we bought at Wal-Mart for only approximately $40 and this recorder has managed to produce many authentic confirmed analyzed EVP's.

Most paranormal researchers also will shy away from the digital recorders that have USB ports in them.

This is because this feature only drives up the cost of the digital recorder and is not a useful function at all because any EVP recordings captured and transferred to computer by USB most of the time somehow appear to be distorted to a sense of sounding mechanical or corrupted in nature. This means that any recordings are usually compromised in some way in that they are destroyed to an aspect that they cannot be used for proper audio evidence in this field. A paranormal researcher will want to buy what is called an audio patch cord to go along with their digital recorder. A patch line in cord can always be purchased at your neighborhood RadioShack store for around $3 or so a cord. Again, I will later explain in another chapter section on EVP's as to how use your digital or analog recorder, patch line, and analyzing computer software to obtain proper recordings and analysis for any possible EVP recordings. There are many right and wrong ways in trying to gather and analyze EVP's.

Another item that every paranormal investigation should have is a digital or 35 mm camera. A person must look at expense here and most digital cameras are very affordable these days. Many paranormal researchers tend to swing more towards purchasing a digital camera because you can take more pictures, see the pictures right away, and not have to deal with the cost of buying film and developing it that is normally associated with 35 mm cameras. When buying a digital camera and using it for paranormal investigative research it is very important that analysis of your pictures be done in the right way. This is because just about every paranormal researcher new to this field will get very excited the first time they start taking pictures in the dark during an investigation. This is because most digital cameras will create what is called the "orb" effect where lots of so-called orbs appear. Most people new to the paranormal investigation will usually feel their hearts beat rapidly as they acquire some pictures of orbs in which they think they have captured spiritual activity. People in the beginning will usually walk around telling other people that they have captured what they think is paranormal activity. The truth of the matter is what is captured is usually only dust or some type of moisture or condensation in the air. This is where there is a pixelation problem that is created on the digital camera in which the camera flash usually reflects off of something like a dust particle or where the shutter actually does not capture all the light and the camera corrects the digital picture by filling in the pixelation with what looks like floating orbs. I have to admit that orbs do not excite me and I unfortunately have had to let many people down by telling the truth of what they think is paranormal activity evidence.

Every paranormal investigator who is really serious to the field of paranormal research should own a SONY camcorder with infrared (nightshot feature) capability and also an additional powered infrared light. This is probably the most essential item of any serious paranormal researcher's arsenal of equipment. An investigator must always have this on them during any investigations because you never quite know what will happen or what might occur. If an event takes place, this makes it that much more probable that the paranormal activity can be captured as evidence to show the rest of the world. There are many SONY brand camcorders out there at many different price ranges. It really does not matter how much you spend, or what exact type of SONY camcorder you purchase, as long as it has the infrared technology in it. Infrared is a feature that many investigators consider very important because we seem to capture more anomalies in the dark than otherwise. Why this happens is not exactly clear, but it is generally believed that if there are any actual ghosts lurking around during an investigation, it is more likely that they will make themselves known in the dark rather than the light. Being in the dark also seems to heighten an investigator's other senses like hearing and smell. This enables an investigator to pick up on more things than he or she would usually do if conducting an investigation with the lights on. As to SONY camcorders, these usually come in many different formats from 8mm, Hi-8, Mini-DV, DVD, Hard-Drive and again it doesn't not really matter what exact format of camcorder an investigator purchases. As time goes on, however, and more technology is available to the public, a lot of these formats will be phased out. Do not forget to purchase an additional individual infrared light to go with your camcorder. This is because that even with your built-in infrared light, the infrared beam on your camcorder is not strong enough to really see anything for any great distance in the dark. The individual infrared light will allow you to capture images in the dark anywhere from at least 35 feet to 60 feet out which will better enable your investigators to capture more possible visual paranormal evidence.

Another important piece of an investigator's main group of equipment is to buy an EMF (Electro-magnetic field) meter. EMF meters are very useful because they will allow you as an investigator to check for any changes in electrical or electromagnetic energy. Every electrical device in a household gives off a certain electromagnetic field around it. Some devices like refrigerators, microwave ovens, televisions, etc. give off very strong EMF field readings and are easily detectable as natural occurrence. When it comes to paranormal investigation, we refer to possible paranormal activity as to being a substantial spike which means that there is a fluctuation in the EMF field as to a change. This means that the spike does not have to be that high for an investigator to take notice. If the spike is too high, than there is a probability of natural phenomena occurring. Investigators in this field have established based on experience that substantial EMF spikes registering anywhere from 5 to 20 miligauss or even a little could possible prove to be paranormal activity, but further analysis and confirmation by other devices also is needed. What paranormal investigators really enjoy about EMF meters is that you can detect electro-magnetic field changes as they move about an environment. In other words, we can detect things possibly moving around us. This may sound strange, but every investigator when they get substantial EMF spikes the first time around will understand better what this all means. You can literally pull a strong EMF spike out of thin air one second and the next second it is gone as quickly as it was there. Sometimes the EMF field per the meter readings will show that the field moves a little to the left or right around the investigative environment.

As to paranormal investigator opinion, it is generally believed that when a spirit or more common term, "ghost" begins to manifest itself within a physical environment, that the form draws off the energy of every item in that area. Paranormal investigators know this as a rule because it is in our experience that our items that hold energy such as batteries, etc. drain easily and quickly when we have had proof of something manifesting. Therefore, there is a differentiation of possible static energy or electric-magnetic energy that creates the EMF spike reading. I will discuss more as to EMF investigation and methods in a later chapter.

Another key piece of paranormal equipment that every investigator should have is a non-contact infrared thermometer. These can range in price anywhere from around $50 to as much as $150. Again, it does not necessarily matter what brand you acquire as long as it provides the right feature that you are looking for. Your infrared non-contact thermometer should reach at least 30 feet within an environment as to capturing temperature changes. The term non-contact means that you can literally stand in one location within a room and register temperature of the whole room from that one location without moving.

This is important because cold or hot spots happen often during paranormal investigations and every investigator needs to be able to register or monitor these substantial temperature changes that are taking place. It is normal that you will have air flow and temperature changes that are natural. Where it becomes un-natural is when it occurs with no natural explanation. This creates the ability to gather sufficient data to concur or back up what your other investigative equipment might be registering within your controlled investigative environment. There are many theories as to what might cause cold or hot spots as to paranormal activity, but again it is generally believed that when a spirit or ghost manifesting itself within a physical environment, that it draws on all the energy around it including the molecules in the air. This change of the electrical charge in the air is believed to either warm or cool the air around it drastically creating either a hot or cold spot. Again, there are several theories to this strange phenomenon, but this is generally the agreed upon theory by experienced paranormal investigators as to why these changes occur. I will go deeper into this possible explanation of what occurs in another section of this book.

# Chapter 4: Finding the Investigation

Many people reading this book will wonder why he put a chapter titled like this in the book. The reality of why this chapter is needed in here for every new paranormal investigator makes for a very strong point. Once a new paranormal investigator has acquired all his or her equipment, then the question is out there of what places can be investigated properly. This is important, because take it from me, finding good investigations to conduct are not easy at all.

A person will usually conduct an internet search or acquire books about the region that he or she lives in as to trying to find confirmed or rumored to be local haunted places to investigate. What is funny here is that once you get on the internet doing this, you will find that there are many folklore legends existing out there in just about every place across America and the world. You will come across many websites out there that will relay the exact same local haunted stories of locations. The question that many face is on how to determine if these reported places are truly worth investigating at all or if these places are even accessible for paranormal investigation. The answer to this question that many new to this field of research will find out here is no.

Now that I have established why I wanted to include this chapter for all to review, I want to explain more as to the importance that every investigator should have as to finding places to investigate properly. There are many right and wrong ways to go about this. Unfortunately, during my years doing this, I have seen many people new to this field go about it all in the wrong ways. This can and usually always does possibly lead to trouble in the forms of breaking the law, someone getting hurt, or you or your investigating team developing a very bad reputation in the paranormal investigation community. One of the worst things that a new paranormal investigator can do is run around cemeteries at night looking for ghosts. This is because many people have loved ones in the cemetery and that the cemetery is really a private place no matter how public it may appear. Someone owns that property and would not be thrilled at all if they knew that people were running all over it late at night doing things like this. Now, there are of course many, what we call haunted cemeteries across the country and the world, and there are many paranormal organizations that do investigate these places properly. The key here is that these organizations contact the owners of these establishments well before the actual investigation is to take place to make sure that legal permission is granted from the owners and that all liability issues have been examined properly.

You will find that there are not many owners of cemeteries who are very fond of paranormal investigators trouncing around their grounds at night doing investigations. Many cemetery owners will not grant permission for things like this on their property and most cemeteries are locked up tight during the nighttime hours. There are, however, some cemeteries out there that are claimed to be haunted and have a mystique about them. The owners of these cemeteries usually will not mind an investigation on their grounds as long as you maintain good contact and permission beforehand.

Many people will form paranormal organizations of their own because of friends and acquaintances they have with a similar interest in the paranormal world of ghosts and hauntings. The question is what do they do once the actual organization is formed? It is much harder to find very good places to investigate than one would think. This is because of the lack of information out there about areas and also competition from other paranormal investigative organizations already established in certain areas. I would recommend to anyone that it is best to get with a paranormal organization that has years experience doing this already. This is because you will learn all aspects of good paranormal investigation and this also will help one to see that this field is not as easy as one would think in finding good places to investigate.

By joining an already well established paranormal organization, a person also will find out all the pros and cons of paranormal investigation that are out there. The more established paranormal organizations are more likely to be better known and trusted within the community as to the investigations they have already conducted. I have gone on the internet many times to various paranormal organizations and looked at the number of actual cases they do each year. There are many paranormal organizations out there where I only see about two or three paranormal investigations a year and many of these do not usually appear to be client related and a lot of them are in cemeteries.

The first thing I would suggest for any new paranormal investigator or organization to do here is take the time to complete some very good research as to the area where they live and are established. This can be done by reading newspaper and magazine articles, and getting on the internet to see what information can be found. It also does not hurt to just go around and ask people what they know. Make a list of all the haunted locations you are able to find in a 50 to 100 mile radius all around your location where you are established and live.

Once you have this list compiled, then do extensive research of each individual place to determine any validity of reports of haunted paranormal activity there and who has already investigated these places. If there are other paranormal teams shown that have investigated and said that the location is haunted, then try to look at their evidence and possibly contact them to ask why they feel the location was haunted. The main thing is to do your own extensive research; do not ever just take another person's word that a location is haunted and that it is a good location to investigate. Take a good look at the actual rumored to be haunted location and determine from your analysis if this is just a legend or so called urban legend. I say this because there are many such places like this in every city or town out there.

Many of the legends seem to live on throughout the ages even though there is no actual documented proof out there that the location has paranormal activity or is haunted. This is because every young generation seems to create the excitement and folklore of the haunted story again. I will give you an example.

I am sure that many people across America have heard the haunted story of some young lady dressed in either black or white walking alongside the road as if she has had some car accident or something. The person stops to lend a hand to this young lady who either gets into the front or back seat. The young lady then states that she has to get home to her house. The person driving then tries to create conversation with the young lady who only seems to stare ahead on the road and not speak another word. The driver starts to think that this young lady looks very white and pale for her color and sometimes appears wet. The driver also sometimes notices that the clothes on this young lady appear to be slightly old-fashioned. Upon arriving at the destination requested by this young woman, this usually being a house, park, school, or possibly a cemetery, the driver then looks over at their passenger to ask them if they are at the correct location. To their shock, the young lady has suddenly vanished without a trace. The person then goes up to the house to ask and is told by the shocked owner that their daughter was killed in a car crash several years ago while attending a school dance or something. Now, I have not gone into every detail of what these stories usually sound like, but this is very close to the urban myth that is passed on from one generation to another in many locations. I am sure that many have heard this story. The story is simply never able to be confirmed by anyone as being true.

A person will find as they go down their list of haunted places that they can quickly eliminate most of the places as being just legends or urban myths. A search on the internet will not turn up anything on these places except just being stories. A lot of these stories just keep getting added to over the years. It is like a person making up a haunted story of a location, and then another person adding to the previous story as they tell it to another person. Pretty soon a community will have a good urban legend haunted story about a particular location and everyone will appear to strongly believe that story even though there has never been any real concrete proof of being haunted. If a paranormal organization chooses to believe in these stories because of inadequate information and wastes their time going to these places to investigate, then that is truly just a waste of time for everyone. A very big example here of another very large urban haunted story legend is the "Ghost Tracks of San Antonio" which has been around for probably at least thirty years.

I had always heard of this story since I was young of the haunted tracks located in San Antonio, Texas, where it was strongly rumored that a school bus of children one day sometime in the 1930's had attempted to cross railroad tracks at a location and stalled on the tracks only to be hit by a train and everyone killed on the school bus. The urban legend goes on that if a person pulls up to these railroad tracks and puts the vehicle in neutral with the engine off, that after a couple of minutes there will be a mysterious pushing motion from behind as if a ghostly other worldly force is pushing on the vehicle to get it off the tracks. A vehicle will start rolling right off the tracks till it is a safe distance away from the tracks and any imminent danger of being hit by a train. These railroad tracks are also still very much traveled by trains.

From a paranormal investigator viewpoint, this story is totally fictitious with no proof what so ever that this catastrophic event ever occurred. There are no newspaper stories out there confirming any such incident. The area around the tracks looks very flat and horizontal which does lead a person to think it would be very strange that a vehicle would be able to roll from a stopped position up and over the tracks. The reality of this story is that I am not going to name the location of the tracks because I and many other paranormal investigators are very tired of this false story circulating around and new people going to the location. I have in the past personally conducted an investigation of this location a few times and determined that even though the area may look flat, it is actually on a degree sloped incline where the sheer gravity force and inertia of physics will cause a vehicle to roll from a stopped position on the tracks to a position up and over and off the tracks on the other side. I have determined in all my past research and analysis that this whole haunted story as grand as it may appear, is just another mere urban legend story passed from one generation of people to another.

Each new generation takes new interest in the story thinking it is true when in fact it is not. It is like a group of children who tell one of the children to go into the dark spooky old abandoned house because it is haunted and no one ever comes out of there after they go in. The normal mental outlook of this child because of the story would be that they are immediately made to be very afraid of this abandoned haunted old house and what resides in it. I use this story here in my example of how an urban legend haunted story can get very out of hand as it is told through the years. I and many other paranormal investigators wish that this San Antonio Ghost Tracks urban legend would die once and for all because of all the dangers it puts people in who go out to this location trying to experience ghosts and a haunted event. There are also people who live by this area of the railroad tracks in San Antonio, Texas, who I imagine must be very tired of all the vehicle traffic and shenanigans that goes on there not to mention that this area is now heavily patrolled by the police for safety reasons.

Again, this example here is something that a good paranormal organization should not do as to wasting good time and energy trying to investigate a made up paranormal haunted story. There will be people who will try to stare me in the face and tell me that the story is very true because they have been there. I will just simply look back at that person and tell them, show me the undeniable proof and of course I never hear back from them. One thing that good paranormal organizations do is search for historic locations with substance as to investigation. There are many guidelines that a paranormal organization needs to go through in trying to get an investigation at a historical site. This can usually take many months of good communication back and forth and of course getting legal permission in writing from the establishment before a paranormal investigation is actually scheduled. Historic places are always very good for a paranormal team to investigate because of certain things that might have happened with the establishment like battles, strange circumstances, etc. Historic places are not usually easy to get into at all as to being able to conduct a controlled overnight paranormal investigation because of several things. They are usually protected by either state or federal laws or that there is simply too much paperwork and review that is needed. The best way to go about this is to look up the historic place online or call them directly. Then look to see who their public relations person is. Then discuss with that person what you or your team's intentions are and what you are hoping to gain from the investigation. After you tell the administrators your intentions, discuss your organization entirely to them and forward documentation such as letterhead, organization email address, business cards, etc. for them to keep.

Every team should also have what is called a liability consent form that both the team signs and the historic location organization signs. This basically means in layman terms that you agree not to sue them if anyone on your team is hurt and that they agree not to sue your team for various things. One thing you must remember with any historic place is pretty clear; respect the property and all items on that property against damage. If you or your team is able to get through all of this paperwork process, being able to conduct a paranormal investigation on the grounds of most of these historic haunted locations will be worth all the time that is needed. Otherwise, you could destroy others' chances of ever investigating there again.

Another type of paranormal investigation that many of us in this field do is what we call client cases. This can involve either individuals or organizations such as businesses. These are usually people who contact your organization claiming to have strange unexplainable occurrences and that they are seeking your organization's aid and assistance for a paranormal investigation to be done. They want to see what you can uncover to confirm what they have experienced and to get your professional opinion and help. It is not often that client cases come forth. A very good paranormal investigation team would be lucky to get two client cases a month. This is because of communication and awareness. In this field, you will soon find that a paranormal organization does not, in reality, want more than two client paranormal investigative cases a month. Two client cases a month may not sound like much, but it is. If a paranormal team takes on something like three to four cases a month if they are somehow available, then that

70

paranormal team will soon realize they are getting too burdened and possibly start to rush the investigations and analysis which results in disaster for both the team and the clients involved. Many people new to the paranormal investigative research field again do not realize how much actual time and dedication is involved with an investigation from start to finish.

When you are contacted by the client seeking a paranormal investigation, there are several initial things that you as an individual investigator or lead team investigator must do for yourself, your team, and the potential client. When a client contacts you whether by phone or email, you must then proceed to gather as much information as possible about the client, their family, their business, and of course the location and what is happening. Take as many initial notes as possible so that you and your team can assess those notes later and so that you can compile a good case report. The main thing to remember when talking with the client in the beginning is that you want to sincerely thank them for contacting you and to also express to the client that you must first gather a lot of information to determine if a paranormal investigation is even needed or warranted. I say this because you do not in the end want to waste the client's time or you or your team's time. If you are conducting paranormal investigations by yourself and do not ask the right questions because you are inexperienced, you could be wasting a lot of time. If you are a lead investigator for an investigative team, then you will be wasting your team's time and they will soon see this and become frustrated and disgruntled.

In speaking with the client, it is generally good to maybe also speak to other family members or associates of the client to see if they have experienced the same kinds of strange experiences. It is not always needed from a reference point to speak with other people at the same location, but in this field it will provide a lot more information to again determine if a location is worth spending the time to investigate and to also get a better idea as to what may be happening in the location. It will provide a well-rounded perception of the location and the history of it. Another important thing that you must secure from the client is the timeframe of unexplainable events that are occurring. This is because you will want to see if there is a large frequency of these events as having just occurred or if they possibly may have occurred several years ago.

If any events have happened a year ago or possibly several years ago and no strange identical unexplained event has occurred since, then chances are that the investigation does not need to be done. You would then have to really review and explain to the client if this is the case. You always want to remain very polite and courteous even if you see that an investigation is not needed. Again, in this field you do not want to waste your clients or your time for any reason. You also want to take good notes as to what exactly has been happening and where in the location these events have occurred and who was present at the time to witness the event. You will need to ask the client to describe to you in great detail as to what they experienced and witnessed. Reassure the client that you need to hear everything and will not think for a moment that any of what they tell you is ridiculous or funny. It's also a good idea to ask your client to keep a log of events that can be used for later analysis. It is even alright to ask the client if it is okay by them for you to record the telephone conversation if you have trouble hearing or writing down all the notes and are afraid that you might miss something. You also during this process will want to do what I in my own words call a psyche-analysis of the given situation and client. Now, I am not a medical doctor and never at any time have I ever proclaimed that I know the things that doctors know, but any person with good practice at any time can get a good feel of what another person says as to their statements, determine if they are telling the truth, and if they are a credible person.

You will also find that many things that you may do in your regular day job may help you and can be applied in the paranormal investigative field. I used to be an insurance claims adjuster and I have in the past taken thousands of recorded statements from people about automobile accidents in conducting my investigations of those insurance claims. In that field, I soon learned the right exact type of questions to ask of people and what key factors to look for in determining if a person is truthfully stating how an accident occurred. I found in the insurance field that many people lie and are fraudulent about facts in accidents on their claims unfortunately which is a big part of human life. You always want to be objective in how you assess any situation when a client does contact you. This all applies to the types of questions you ask as a paranormal investigator to your client. Make sure you have your list of formatted written questions that you ask each and every time of any potential client. You may deviate from some of these questions because of what you hear from the client, and you may come up with some new questions due to those situations. You never want to make your client feel like they are being interrogated or being put in the spotlight so to speak, but you do want to develop a good enough relationship with them where they are not afraid to speak quite freely with you about what they have experienced or witnessed.

You will need to cover the who, what, where, when, and how of the presented situation. If you conduct yourself professionally on the phone as to sincerely and truthfully wanting to help them, then that client should feel very comfortable around you and your team later. Always remember that we as investigators are primarily in this research field to help other people and ourselves understand more as to the paranormal world of ghosts and hauntings, not for our own personal gain or glory.

# Chapter 5: Conducting the Paranormal Investigation

Now it is time for a group or team to move towards conducting an actual paranormal investigation. There are steps here. Once you have gathered all of your information for either a client investigation or if you are looking to do your own investigation of a selected location, then it is very important to do some actual research of the location. This will involve gathering any history of the location that can be found and determine how long the structure has been there and what occurred with it over the years. This is where the internet can help you tremendously. In the old days, we only had libraries to try to search out this kind of information which took a long time to do with many unsuccessful results.

Now we readily have a lot of pertinent information at the simple touch of a finger on our computers. If you are doing an individual client investigation, this will involve checking land deed records of the owner and previous owner's history, checking city newspaper articles to see if anything occurred at that location or address, and doing other very extensive internet research of information. Internet searches would involve thinking of the appropriate key words to see if any fact information can be returned. You will find a lot of times that you hit a dead end here, but the same protocol of gathering research needs to be done each and every time for every case investigation. You will find that every so often you can find a goldmine of information that can be used to sort out what is found during the paranormal investigation such as names, history, and so forth. Every good and successful paranormal investigation team out there will have its own lead researcher/historian who conducts this intelligence information gathering and creates the research folder.

Before any team can conduct any paranormal investigation, that team must have good leadership and organization. Each and every team member should have a certain authority and responsibility within that team. The overall strength of how well that paranormal team does things and performs on investigations is based on how well everyone on the team adapts to each other for their individual roles. The founders and experienced people of the team will of course have the lead investigator roles within the team. A person on any paranormal team should not be unwilling to follow in someone else's footsteps as to learning the rights and wrongs of doing proper paranormal investigation. Any person who has just begun doing paranormal investigation or having just joined a prominent paranormal team should be very willing to follow orders. If there is any tension in this area with anyone on the team, then there will be future problems that will undermine the effectiveness of the whole team production. I have seen so many team organizations out there where everyone on the team just runs carelessly around the location trying to do their own individual investigations and not follow any set guidelines. What I don't understand about people like this in general is why they wanted to join a paranormal team in the first place. A word of advice in this field is that if you cannot get along with other people within a team environment and you do not like following orders, then team paranormal investigation is not the thing for you.

Another very important position within the team that should be created is the Team Tech Manager. This team position has to require that someone know a lot about the equipment set up and take down, know techniques as to setting up equipment, have extensive investigating experience, and overall respect from the whole team. This position involves a lot of cut and chase to get the investigation completed in a timely fashion. Other investigators should all help out with set up and take down of all the equipment, but the Lead Investigators and Tech Manager have the final say on how everything is done. The rest of the positions on the team should just be for investigators and other things like public relations, etc. It really does not matter how you organize the team as long as everyone knows that the organization role names are only as good as getting the job done right each and every time. It should never be about one person being better than another person on the team and that sort of negative talk and energy.

Everyone is there for the same reason as to completing the cases and mission. Every team should also have a good organization team mission statement as to what they provide for and follow it no matter what. It is always good to have a rules, ethics, and conduct bylaws that everyone on the team reads, acknowledges, signs, and abides by. This way if someone does violate something such as to conduct or ethics rules within the team, then you as the leader can provide them with a solid reason why you are warning or letting them go from the team. There should be no surprises of what behavior is expected while anyone is working on the team. Another thing that I highly recommend is that you should have a clear statement in the conduct and ethics form that states quite specifically that no one on the team has the right to investigate with any other paranormal teams or disseminate any privileged confidential client case information to any parties outside of the paranormal team. This is for the safety and privacy of the client. Even though there are usually no paid positions within a paranormal organization team, it should show that there will always be rules and conduct that need to be followed each and every time by the members of the team. Once a paranormal team has everything defined and organized, that team will function as a well-oiled machine each and every paranormal investigation and the results will show for all to see.

Every good paranormal team should also have their own developed professional organization website. I am not talking about a main site on either MySpace, Face book, or other free social websites out there on the internet. It is also good to have a alternative MySpace, Facebook, or other site up somewhere for media advertising and networking purposes, but you should not rely on these for your main contact purposes and advising the world who you are. Your main developed website should be your direct communication source to the public. This should be a developed organization website that is compatible and searchable as to all the search engines and web browsers on the internet. Make sure that you cover all the paranormal and your location keywords out there when you develop, create, and publish your website to the internet. A person may think that clients will start hitting their website and will be contacting them frequently, but they will soon find out that business dwindles because of a lack of advertising as to who you are, what you do, and how long you have done it. That is what networking is all about. You have to show the world and the potential clients as to why your team may be the better choice to the client than the next paranormal team down the block when they pull up all the internet results as to their search for assistance.

When clients do searches looking for a good paranormal team to assist them, they get all sorts of hits on the internet and are easily confused by what they see due to maybe not using the right search keywords. What I am stating here is that your overall experience, knowledge, work, and name should speak for itself to anyone when they locate your website and organization. If I was a client and found a paranormal team out there with only a free MySpace, Face book, or other social website as their only main contact source, I would probably walk the other way. There should never be any bashing, competition, or disrespectful things said of any other paranormal teams in your area. You will find after many years if you are still in this field at that time, that your name will later become known to the public and other paranormal researchers in this field and you will receive new business and case referrals from time to time if no one is available in the area where an investigation is requested. This will not happen overnight as to attracting clients and support of your organization.

The reality is that some very good paranormal teams have had the good fortune and luck as to getting their own shows and fan bases. They however did this with a lot of hard work and time. This is great because I know a lot of these fellow investigators personally and wish them the best for what they have done and contributed to this field up till this time, but the stone cold reality for many in this research field is that day will never come where we all have the time and opportunity to have a great paranormal show like Ghost Hunters, Ghost Hunters International, Paranormal State, Ghost Adventures, Most Haunted, and Ghost Lab, etc. In time due to many reasons, the seasons and episodes for these shows will end, but these paranormal organizations will carry on just like they always have as to helping people and researching the paranormal world of ghosts and hauntings.

These paranormal organizations are very well known due to their television exposure and usually do not have any problems at all having clients contact them directly for assistance and guidance. There are only so many television cable/satellite networks out there and just about every one of them already has some kind of paranormal investigation or haunting show on it. The television networks are not looking for any copy cats, they are looking for originality that attracts large amounts of viewers and consumers to their networks. The fact here is that there are many well respected names in this field, some have paranormal television shows, and some do not. I do know a few of these famous television celebrity paranormal investigators personally. They are still good friends and regular people just like you and me. Without having to name anyone in particular, I have also seen some teams out there form up for the sole purpose of trying to get a television show and become famous just to attain that celebrity status, have their fans, and profit from the venture. I have to say that this is not what the true paranormal investigation research field is about. What most people do not realize from the paranormal television shows is that these paranormal team organizations help a lot of clients and devote a lot of their time and behind the scene background preparation as to making sure that each investigation is a success. In the end, the paranormal investigative research field is a very difficult field to become accustomed to and can be very exhaustive.

Now that I have talked about the ins and outs of determining team organization, let's now discuss how to properly prepare and conduct an investigation once you have taken on your first paranormal case. This may sound easy, but it again is not. Any paranormal teams in the beginning are not going to initially realize that the client is going to have very high expectations of your team and what will be discovered during the investigation. The clients will have a very high anxiety level due to this which is a normal human response to something like this. Many clients also may strongly feel that a paranormal team has the means to exterminate and do away with what may be in their house or business. A paranormal team in the beginning must also have the objective mentality that you will conduct your investigation to see what you can find out and not just base everything solely on what the client states. This is not to discredit any client out there, but in the beginning these are just statements and stories that the client is telling you as the paranormal investigator. You have not yet been able

80

to determine for yourself any validity of the client's claims of paranormal activity in their home or business. For now, the initial client's claims will and are the basis of how you will set up your equipment for the investigation to be conducted.

When a client discusses what has happened, remember that you should have already taken good notes and done your own individual synopsis as to determining where in the location the strange activity has occurred and what game plan you will initiate for the investigation. When you personally meet with your client for the first time, you must sit down to discuss with them your team strategy and investigation process for that night's investigation. You must and should also legally complete what is called a liability release consent form. This is a legal form letter that you can find a few versions of on the internet and you should have the basis legal language in it along with your paranormal organization's name stating that basically you agree not to sue the client for anything that occurs during the course of you being on their property and that the client will not sue you or hold your organization accountable for anything that happens or any claims of property being taken from the client's property. This can be worded any way you want must contain the legal statements in this capacity so as to protect everyone in your organization and also protect the client. You should have name, position, and signature blocks for each member of your team investigating that night on the location and also have a name/signature block for the consenting property location owner to sign as well. This form should officially be dated as well.

Another recommended form you can have and give to the consenting property owner is what is called a Feedback/Referral form that the owner completes after the investigation and reveal for the client have been done. This is so that the client has their opportunity to provide their opinion and thoughts as to how your paranormal organizations services were and offer their name as a referral in case your organization would need to provide to someone else.

Once you have completed all of the necessary required forms and discussed everything as to the investigation process with the client, you know want to begin walk-through. This is a process where the lead investigators of your organization do a walk-through with the client so that the client can again describe in detail the locations of the property location where the supposedly unexplained paranormal activity occurred to them or other witnesses. You should again make notes of these locations and decide in your head while doing the walk-through as to where you will position all of your cameras as to these hot spots. A hot spot in paranormal investigation communication lingo is an area in a property location where the alleged strong paranormal activity occurred.

Once the walk-through is done, you should then advise the client that you need to lock down the premises as to doing a controlled investigation. This involves having the client and all family members leave the location. You should have also already explained to the client in the beginning as to your initial phone call interview as to this process needing to be done so that your team has a better chance of capturing unexplained paranormal activity due to there being no contamination from the client of the gathered evidence obtained.

If a client does not initially feel comfortable as to leaving you or your team alone in the premises of their home or business for the night, then you can always work something out where only the owner of the property is present for the investigation, but again you should strongly advise that client that it is best that no one other than the team is present for the investigation for the best results. This is also needed so that the client is not able to hear the opinions or statements of the paranormal investigators present or possibly influence the activities of the investigators during the course of the investigation. This is not a negative thing in the least because we again as investigators want to help the client but must remain openly objective to any claims of paranormal activity by the client. We want the ability to see for ourselves as investigators as to what actually occurs in a location so that we can later confirm it with client accounts of what occurred. We also want to rule out by deduction, review, and the analysis process which is called debunking if what is occurring in the property location can be determined to be caused by any possible natural means. I will further explain this debunking process later where I discuss evidence analysis process in greater detail. It basically means that we as investigators must use every means and open mind to determine if any accounts by the client are naturally occurring.

The next step after the initial walk-through of your client's home or business is to get with your Tech Manager and team as to discussing the case more and the setup. Walk them through the house or business and tape x marks with duct tape as to the spots where you would like your cameras to be positioned. You should, as the lead investigator, already have assembled in your head as to the placement of the video cameras so you can accurately cover on video all the active hot spots within the environment. You want to make sure that you also have all the camera lens angles positioned just right so that you do not mistakenly miss any area during the investigation. If your video cameras are not positioned just right, you might have blown a good opportunity to capturing evidence that night and in the meantime wasted a lot of everyone's time. You could also blow a perfectly executed investigation.

You also want to position extra video cameras from good vantage points throughout the location such as hallways or walkways etc.; this is why a good DVR camcorder system is needed with several camera units. A four channel DVR IR camera system will do the job without any problems, but there are also paranormal organizations out there using eight channel and larger for their DVR systems. The problem with using a larger channel DVR system is that your review screen will get smaller with each camera view if you are trying to look at all of your cameras at the same time.

With a four channel DVR IR camera system, you have four rather large screens that are large enough to be viewed quite easily throughout the course of the investigation. This type of a system will also give your team more eyes within the environment as to detecting anything. This is especially needed within large environments that you need to cover for review. One thing I like about using DVR IR camera systems is that a person can notice that a lot of activity happens while an investigator might possibly be leaving a room or when their head is turned the other way. These camera systems give us more opportunity in this field to catch unseen paranormal activity when investigator eyes do not.

There are several different types of DVR camera systems on the market with different pricing. It really comes down to what you want exactly and what you are willing to spend as to the kind of system you get. It is however good to get a DVR system that already has a built in DVD burner unit installed in it, so that you can burn DVD's as to your collected video evidence. You also want to have a DVR system that is easy as to recording, rewinding, and forwarding on your camera unit footage. There are also a lot of systems out there where you can implement live website investigation feed for the public and your fans with the use of a PC hooked to your system. These types of systems may be a little more, but are worth it in the end. Range of pricing on good DVR IR camera systems can range anywhere from $800 to $3000 depending on what you are looking for or needing.

You also want to make sure that you have tri-pods for each of your individual cam units. The camera tri-pods can vary in size, but you want to have large tri-pods as well as smaller ones so that you can put individual cam units on shelves, bookcases, etc. in getting the right angle views of the hotspots within the investigation location. An important thing to remember here is to purchase hundreds of feet of cable and cable rollers so that you can easily link all your cam units to the DVR system and make sure that none of your cables get tangled up. Once connected, make sure that you teach your team how to properly run the cables throughout the location and tape the cable lines down with duct tape or something so that no accidents occur while the investigation is taking place. You will go through a lot of tape in the end, but it is worth it due to safety factors. If someone trips one of your cam unit lines in the dark due to it not being securely fastened, then you will have the high cost of buying a new cam unit which you definitely want to avoid.

While setting up the DVR system and the camera units throughout the investigation site, a team would then have to establish a control station somewhere either inside or outside the location. If you are setting up inside, you need to choose a room furthest away from the cameras and hotspots that you are investigating. This is so that contamination of the film and audio footage does not take place. This room should have a door that can be closed off to further enable sound silencing. Remember that your control station is the heart of the investigation. Investigators will come and go from this location over and over again to retrieve and put back equipment. Different investigators should also monitor the DVR video screen at all times for signs of any unexplained paranormal activity. Different people are needed during the course of the investigation so that no one investigator gets tired throughout the night where important things are accidently missed.

Each individual cam unit should be numbered and a log should be prepared and used where an investigator will log the exact time and cam unit number each time something strange is observed. This is so the team can go back to specific points of observance as to analyzing the video footage to determine if what was seen can be determined to be paranormal activity of just naturally occurring. It is also good to use a walkie-talkie communication system where the video observer can then communicate to any investigators near the area of the strange activity so that they can go to that area in hopes of capturing or witnessing more activity. The walkie-talkie is very important for the whole team as to having an effective investigation. It will help cut down on a lot of unwanted walking around, noise, and further verification of any activity occurring. When an investigator does experience something, they may also want to communicate back and forth with the control base station to see if more assistance can be rendered without that investigator having to leave the area they are assigned to as to investigating and also to not disturb what may be occurring at that moment. A good walkie-talkie system with good receiving range is a definite must for any paranormal organization to have and use.

In the beginning of the paranormal investigation, the lead investigator will determine and designate who will investigate together on a team, what areas of the location they will investigate together, what type of equipment the investigators should be investigating with at that particular time, what types of investigating experiments might take place, and how many actual teams will go out at any given time to investigate, and what duration of time these investigators will investigate for before they come back to the base control station. This is very important that all of this is noted and done at the very beginning of the investigation so that there is a controlled and uncontaminated environment within the location during the course of the whole investigation. There must be order for any good investigative paranormal team to succeed at trying to get good evidence. Another very important point here is also for all investigators on a team to know that it is the regular and efficient practice as to tagging anything heard during the investigation.

Every time an investigator hears or experiences something they should immediately verbally tag that situation whether by audio or video as to being determined to be naturally occurring or possibly paranormal activity. If this process is not done right each and every time by a paranormal team during an investigation, then all of the possible captured evidence will be literally deemed useless and contaminated. It is also a must that no one on the team ever whispers at all when they speak. If a person has to speak, please make sure that every word is said in normal speech manner. If people are speaking at the control base station and an investigator for some reason hears something, then that investigator should immediately tag the situation on audio or video and get on their walkie-talkie to check with the control station to determine if someone was speaking or making some other noise at the time. Contamination of evidence is one of the worst things that can happen for any paranormal team because you can lose hours of investigation time if the right processes are not followed by the team.

When a paranormal team starts their investigation, they must create as much of a controlled environment as they can. This involves making sure that all windows and doors are closed and sealed, that any air conditioner or ceiling fans are turned off, that all lights are turned off, and that every team investigator is where he or she must be as to given assignment. A team must have all cooling or heating sources off so as to be better enable detection of cold or hot spots within the location environment. In the beginning of the investigation, there should be a base temperature and EMF (electro-magnetic field) sweep done by investigators of the whole location to determine the baseline given temperatures of each room and also if there are any high EMF fluctuations present and what their source might be from. This is to ensure that if there are any other substantial changes in temperature or EMF fields detected in the location, and then this available additional information can help the investigators analyze and try to figure out if those changes are deemed to be paranormal or naturally occurring.

Duration of the investigation period and the time of the investigation starting are up to the paranormal investigation team to decide. There is no right or wrong here to do this. A paranormal team should allow at least an hour before an investigation begins for proper set up and placement of all the equipment. This is so that no one has to rush the investigation. I have found that many clients are willing to turn their house or property over during the investigation hours and then leave and come back later. Other clients will sometimes wait outside for the team to complete everything.

Typically most investigations by teams are started around 10:00 P.M. and end around 3:00 to 4:00 A.M. This is because, for unknown reasons to paranormal investigators, most paranormal activity seems to occur during those hours and more so closer to 2:00 or 3:00 A.M. or possibly even later into the early morning hours. You will hear some stories out there where some will state that 3:00 A.M. is the Devil's Hour or the time that the dead spirits are more prevalent to walk the earth in our physical dimension, but there has been no truth found with this and it still is relatively unknown why these hours are the best for paranormal research to be done as to evidence being gathered. I personally tend to believe that the hours around 2:00 A.M. to 5:00 A.M. tend to be the early morning hours when the mind and body of a person are well rested and calmed down enough where people will possibly be more psychically receptive to seeing or experiencing paranormal phenomenon during that time period. Many people appear to be the most relaxed at these hours of their sleep in the night and many stories are out there where people appear to experience strange haunting things around those hours. There does appear to be a window here within those hours where haunting spirit activity is very high and more likely to occur. Again, there is no direct correlation of facts as to what I am stating here, but through all my years experience doing this, most unexplained haunting phenomenon does seem to occur around these hours of the night for some reason.

Before a team starts an investigation, you want to make sure that each and every person has had their share of rest enable the entire senses alert and render a better experience and investigation. Make sure that no one on the investigation team is on any medication or under the influence of alcohol the night of the investigation. As the night and investigation progresses, changes to the individual investigation teams and methods throughout the night will be made according to what is experienced or seen.

There is a number one rule with paranormal investigation, which is to never investigate alone. This is for pure safety if someone gets hurt so that first aid can be administered to that person and everyone is aware of the incident. If paranormal activity is witnessed or experienced, than a person will have the second associate investigator present there to help confirm, correlate, and share information.

Another very important process to implement during the actual investigation is what is called debunking. This is a process by which investigators will disseminate information between themselves that the client has provided which will help to determine if anything experienced or witnessed by the client or their family can be determined as to being naturally induced or occurring. Remember I said earlier that each and every investigator must have an objective or skeptical stance in the beginning of any investigation. Even if a client states all kinds of strange things have happened or have been seen, a paranormal team must just take note of all of this information and go through a debunking process each and every time to see if there is validity to the client's claims. This is not to discredit the client in any manner, but to help explain to them if naturally occurring things are indeed found by the team. In the paranormal investigation field, there are only approximately 10% of cases where it is seen that true unexplained paranormal activity occurs which is a very small number of cases.

If a paranormal investigation team does ten cases one by one, then only one of those cases will have some degree of strong confirmed unexplained paranormal phenomenon happening. The investigation individual teams should all take turns doing the debunking process on each of the client's claims to see if anything can be explained naturally. This involves recreating the events that the client described. During the investigation, if anything out of the ordinary is witnessed or experienced by the individual investigation teams, then a debunking process should also be done to see if the unexplained events can be recreated in any fashion as to being proven a natural event. This is a very common practice when any strange noises or shadows are seen by an investigation team. Every strange experience should be documented and everything that was done to try to debunk what had happened should be written and carefully noted for later review. A good paranormal investigator should be skeptical of all of their work as to all the evidence that is found to provide a basis to rule out all possible naturally occurring things and to accurately prove to someone who was not present from a scientific foundation that any captured paranormal activity evidence is credible and supported at the same time by at least two sources of paranormal equipment. It is like when we witness a light bulb being turned on. We know what our eyes are seeing and our mind is reasoning as to the light bulb turning on, but how do we prove from a scientific vantage point to another person as to how and why that light bulb is turning on.

The debunking process that paranormal investigators use should be complex where all things are checked and verified carefully one step at a time on a highly skeptical level. This would be similar to what is used to disprove something. Debunking involves a breakdown methodology where the gathered information is taken apart piece by piece and analyzed thoroughly for any discrepancies. At the same time all of this is being done, a good solid paranormal investigator should never be too skeptical of the gathered evidence and the whole team's efforts where good possible evidence ends up being ignored and never realistically analyzed from a whole team opinion or believed as to being credible.

The last two steps of any paranormal investigation are to complete a review and analysis of all the gathered evidence and to then provide a structured reveal session for the client as to what was found. Each paranormal investigator should contribute here in looking at what audio and video information was gathered. It is important to have a collective team effort at this phase of the investigation that is completed both quickly and efficiently. There are going to be many very slow nights of investigation where investigators are going to think that they have not acquired anything and then proceed to procrastinate and not want to go through all of their review of the information. A lot of times there are hours and hours of video that needs to be looked at very carefully which can simply be exhausting for anyone. It can also be exhausting to go over the collected audio information. Many investigators work other regular jobs during the week and also have to tend to their family. It is hard for any paranormal investigator to keep up with everything. This is why it's not a good idea to have more than two controlled investigations per month. Investigators simply cannot get through the evidence. Paranormal investigations are some of the hardest work out there because of the all time restraints involved. Every paranormal team should also strongly encourage each individual investigator on the team to have their analysis and evidence submitted within a few days if your team is handling many cases a month. This is important because paranormal investigation teams have their clients to serve and a team will want to stay on top of everything and provide the information and possible evidence to the client in a timely fashion. You will find that the clients are very anxious to see what your team found.

Upon leaving a client's home or business the night of the investigation, a paranormal team should advise the client of what to expect and when the team will get back to them for their reveal. Never ignore or leave a client in the dark as to this information. I give my team five days to do this because we have made it where we only will do up to two investigations a month. There might be some months where we will do three to four a month but this is uncommon due to the big time factor involved. October is usually a very big, busy month that involves back to back investigations and public events. It's a good idea not to overextend the team or its services.

When looking at audio information, it is very important that a paranormal investigation team have the required audio analyzing software. There are many audio programs out there to use, but I have used Adobe Audition now for years and this is still the premiere analyzing software for my organization. The software is very easy to use. I will later explain more about analyzing techniques and how to properly analyze gathered audio recordings for credible EVP's (Electronic Voice Phenomenon). When it comes to doing either video or audio analysis, there really is no easy or quick way, I say just do it. When looking at video segments, I recommend that a person only sits and watches the video for two hour sessions due to possibly becoming tired. Take breaks between video sessions because the eyes can easily become tired and an investigator can miss important paranormal activity evidence due to this factor. Document the exact times, where located, and the camera number. Also review any notes from the night's investigations as to what was noted, so that those sections can be reviewed carefully.

Once everything is looked closely and documented in the case file, then it is always good to have a team meeting where all the supposedly gathered evidence is reviewed. A paranormal team must do a consensus of what each investigator thinks and sees as to the gathered evidence. It is always a good idea that the whole team votes on what they think is evidence and what is not and should be thrown out. As an investigator, never be afraid to state all your points but always be receptive to accept what you have may not be strong enough to be used as actual evidence. We must all remember as an investigator, that the evidence used and presented must be clear and concise enough for the client with untrained eyes and ears to see or hear. The evidence used should be good enough that the client can see or hear it quite clearly and be able to form their own opinion of what is presented to them.

A good paranormal team should first show each piece of evidence to the client before telling the client what the team sees or thinks during the reveal. Let the client see and form their own opinions and then you can discuss your professional investigative opinion and analysis with them. Let the client openly know what the team did during the investigation, how you did your analysis process, and what you think and suggest as the next recourse of action. During the reveal session, it is also very important not to mislead, scare, or worry the client in any way. Always be very careful as to the selection of words you use during discussion with the client. We have to remember that the client either lives or works at that location, and we as paranormal teams should stay away from the wrong terms like stating a demonic entity possibly is present, etc. I say this because I have found from assisting clients who had other previous investigators or teams investigate their home or business only to incorrectly conduct the process, ignore the client after the investigation, or proceed to tell the client with no presentable collected evidence that they think a demon or dark force is present in the client's home.

Good paranormal researchers in this field do know from experience that true demonic haunting cases do exist, but that these cases are very rare and a lot of credible evidence is needed first before a paranormal investigator can even lean towards this opinion as to using that term. I just want to say here that stating this type of stuff prematurely to clients without substantial proven undeniable evidence is just wrong in this field and the good investigation teams soon learn who the bad teams out there are. There are a few demonologists in this field who study and research this sort of thing and who along with strong corroboration and review along with good experienced paranormal teams are the authorities who should comment on this subject. Finally, it is always a good given practice in this field to present a case investigative report of all your observations, findings, and copies of the discussed audio and video evidence for the client to keep for their records

# Chapter 6: Analysis and Methods of Communication

There are many theories and methods of possible afterlife communication and analysis that can be done by a paranormal investigator trying to provide very good credible paranormal activity evidence to the public world. The most common form of paranormal evidence presented by paranormal investigation teams are audio recordings which are called EVP's (Electronic Voice Phenomenon). Some paranormal teams really take an interest in doing really good EVP research and collecting very credible recordings, while other investigators concentrate on other areas of this field. For the person new to paranormal researcher, discovering Electronic Voice Phenomenon can be a very exciting experience and can leave an everlasting feeling of wanting and needing to find out more about what is happening when that first EVP is caught.

I, as a researcher, have acquired many very good clear EVP's over the years that while conducting research in this field. Even though I have captured many very good EVP's over the years, I can still remember one of the first clear undeniable EVP's that I captured. I had been in a cemetery of a very dear friend I had known for many years who had passed suddenly over the course of months from a sudden disease. I had not really been able to say goodbye to her when she was sick and had these thoughts when I was at her funeral. I wished that I could have had that opportunity. One day in the cemetery upon my visit to her grave site, I decided to take my digital audio recorder with me.

I had been doing paranormal research already over a year not professionally, and had not captured a good EVP yet and was not sure if I even believed in EVP research at that time. I had read a lot about the subject and I was sitting on the fence about the whole thing up to that time. I started my digital audio recorder while I talked to her at her gravesite. I remember telling her things like how much I missed her, how I wished I could have said goodbye to her, and wished I had known how very sick she was before she finally passed away suddenly. I went home later and listened to the recording and to my surprise in the first five minutes of the recording; I could hear her voice telling me "Baby, I am okay". There were only four spoken words and the voice was really clear. This was the way she talked to me while she was living; it was the way she talked to people. I played it over and over again to make sure it was her and finally came to the conclusion that it was her voice. I then realized the importance of the EVP section in this field as to what it provides.

Many people will ask why I and my wife are able to get so many very good EVP's. I really do not know the answer to this except to say that I believe that I and my wife are more susceptible to getting a good EVP due to possibly the spirits being very comfortable in speaking with us. It could also be that maybe we are sensitive through our work to the other side to a degree in our ability to acquire some really good EVP communication. A lot of our EVP's literally sound like a real person talking right along with our own voices on audio.

Some of the EVP's that we have acquired over the years have even been said by a few skeptics to be fraudently created. As a very dedicated paranormal researcher in this field, I can definitely state that none of our gathered paranormal evidence is fraudulent or fabricated in any manner and all of our evidence is very real and credible. When some skeptics hear EVPs, they simply want to ignore what they are hearing and immediately try to find a natural cause of it even though our EVP's were captured under very controlled environments and were strongly analyzed by us to ensure that they were not created by natural means. We scrutinize our EVP evidence before it is presented to the public for their opinion. Many years ago, I on my digital audio recorder that was stationary on a table, captured a very good EVP at the very haunted Myrtle's Plantation in St. Francisville, Louisiana where three disembodied voices are heard over our own voices in one of the rooms there. Each of the disembodied voices are also very clear of a grown woman shouting out, a girl asking for help, and a grown elderly man stating something that sounds something like pay the grim reaper. The captured voices are so clear on the recording speaking over our own voices that they are scary sounding.

In explaining Electronic Voice Phenomenon, I must first make clear about what this term is, how it is associated, and how it is used in this research field as to being good confirmed paranormal evidence. I also want to provide a synopsis history of this mysterious area of paranormal research and how it came to be. There were some pioneers to this area of research that were known for their other contributions to the natural science field. A very famous inventor very well known to us gave us many common everyday things including the electric light bulb, the phonograph, and other devices. His name was Thomas Edison and he was not a quack in any manner so to speak by any means as to everything he has provided to the modern science world. He believed in communication that the dead was possible and this could have been for the fact that he maybe had a paranormal experience or accidently in his other personal research witnessed paranormal activity occurring. We really do not know what actually greatly inspired him to dedicate himself so strongly in this area of research later in life.

It is believed by many people that he created a machine that was capable of speaking and communicating with the dead. Thomas Edison would never formally announce his device to the public scientific world as to testing if it actually worked or not, but there were strongly made claims that he was in the final stages of completing the device when he died and that the device was capable of establishing contact and communication with the other side.

I have to take the time to honor those pioneers to the EVP research field for what they brought to this field in their work. There are actually many people who have contributed to this field of research and I tip my hat for what their true perseverance and dedication was. If I started talking here about all the people who have contributed to this field, it would be an entire chapter of listing all of their information. There are many reference materials out there that list who these many researchers are and what they have provided. These people both living and deceased know who they are and what contributions they have provided to this research field. Without these pioneers who were publicly highly criticized and scrutinized for their work, the field of EVP research would not be where it is today. It is because of them that paranormal researchers are at the plateau that we are at today. With modern devices not yet available to the early pioneers of the EVP research study field, we are now able to look even further into the depths and the mysterious world of communication with the other side, or dead as is more commonly referred. It is because of many people's hard work that we are where we are today as to EVP research.

For the beginning paranormal researcher or even for the seasoned researcher already in this field, I wanted to explain how easy it is to do EVP research and analysis. There is a right and a wrong way to doing investigation as to capturing EVP's. I must also state here my own personal definition of Electronic Voice Phenomenon. There are many definitions out there and they are all generally the same with no right or wrong. Electronic Voice Phenomenon is disembodied voices or sound responses captured on electronic audio recording devices which are generally not heard initially when questions are asked by investigators. A paranormal team should conduct several EVP recording sessions which will be only about ten to fifteen minutes. This is to better be able to analyze all the audio recordings for what may be on them.

A paranormal team should have a strongly controlled environment when an EVP session is conducted. There will unfortunately be outside environment noises that cannot be blocked out. A good team needs to 'tag' any natural sound occurring by stating a verbal response every time something natural occurs. If a team does not tag their audio recordings, then a team will not know during analysis if it is a real EVP or not. Therefore, a paranormal team could not use the recordings as evidence and would have to throw out everything.

A good paranormal team should and will also know where every investigator is at the time the EVP session is taking place and there generally will be one lead investigator conducting and leading everything as to the questions. Every team should have their general types of formatted questions to ask and should also ask questions that somehow characterize and have to do with the actual location that is being investigated. For example, if a historic place is being investigated, a team should do some previous historic research and ask questions of what historic figures were maybe at or died at that historic site. This way you can have specific correlated questions to ask to see if an intelligent and meaningful response is captured.

Another thing that a paranormal investigator should do is never be embarrassed to speak out like you would to another person. You want to speak and ask your questions normally as if you are conducting a conversation with someone. You want to sound as natural with your questions as you possibly can and believe in yourself while asking the questions. In other words, do not be skeptical of yourself or overly anticipating if anything will be captured or found out. This does take some practice before you become smooth and comfortable with doing that. Another very important method to follow is to allow at least ten seconds between your asked questions to allow for a captured response and make sure that everyone on your team knows the proper protocol of not just speaking out during the recording session. Also, never whisper during a paranormal investigation. If you have something to say or do, say or announce it loudly as you normally would. This way you do not think that a captured whisper or movement noise is an EVP.

During an investigation, it is generally a good rule to conduct several EVP sessions within a location and it is good to have different directed people taking turns asking the questions. It is also good practice to have several digital audio recordings going at once during the session. This way a team upon analysis can determine if a possible EVP is authentic by seeing if it was captured on any other audio digital recorders at the time and if it sounds differently on those recorders. This helps a paranormal team to see and rule out if the EVP was possibly naturally occurring. The funny thing about real authentic EVP recordings is that a paranormal team will usually find that only one recorder out of many present recorders actually captured the EVP, even though they were all recording at the same time in the location. This will go to prove later that the captured EVP is indeed a strange occurrence and very authentic. If a voice or natural occurring noise were happening, then it would be logical to think that all the recorders should have picked up on that same voice or noise. An experienced team will be amazed to find that there is a high percentage of the time that authentic EVP's are captured on different investigator audio recorders at different times during an investigation.

Now, I have had many people ask me as an investigator if I personally believe that captured EVP's are real spiritual disembodied voices or noises from beyond or the other side as they say. I have to say again that due to all the EVP's I have captured over time, the strange communication things that have been said on the EVP's, and the locations of where the EVP's were captured, that yes – I do strongly believe these audio recordings are communicating voices of the dead or spiritual world which is my personal opinion being an investigator after all these years in this field. I know that it is a very strong statement to make or believe, but I have gotten over the years far too many of these very clear strange disembodied voices and noises on recording to think otherwise. I believe that every investigator in this field is skeptical of EVP's until that investigator has captured their first really clear Class A EVP recording.

Investigators will find at that time that they cannot effectively explain that recording any way that they look at it. I have had other investigators in this field try to criticize the EVP's that I captured, and then I ask them if they have ever obtained anything extraordinary like what I have gotten. I always find that skeptical investigators like this cannot ever produce an equal or comparable EVP of their own at this level because they have never been able to get an authentic EVP. I also believe that an investigator must have an open mind in trying to capture authentic EVP's. If an investigator does not sincerely believe in what they are doing when carrying on effective EVP research, then of course you will never get anything. It is like an astronaut not believing that space travel is possible even though you are about to blast off on a rocket into space. I do see that the people who do not have open minds usually turn out to be the skeptics that carefully try to scrutinize and disprove every aspect of this area of paranormal research.

Once a paranormal investigation has been completed, the next important step is to conduct proper analyzing of all the gathered audio data to see if any paranormal activity is present. This is much harder than it seems because of what is involved as to time and dedication. When an investigation is conducted with say a team of five investigators for four or five hours on many audio digital recorders, this means that there will be several hours (at least 20 hours) of audio data that needs to be reviewed carefully. Each investigator has their own recorders and sole responsibility as to making sure that the analyzing is done the same way and correctly each time. I have seen investigators in this field mess up here tremendously when it comes to doing EVP research. This is because they tend to get very lazy after awhile and soon do not follow the right protocol methods. I have even believed and seen that some investigators do not even listen to all of their audio data correctly the way they should and then simply state that they did not get any audio evidence during the investigation. I have come across many dictated methods by people in this field about how to do effective EVP research. I do personally think that the same general rules need to be followed each and every time for an investigator to find authentic EVP's. These disembodied voices and noises sometimes can be very clear and sometimes they can be very hard to hear due to the different sound levels. I do have to say that authentic EVP's happen very infrequently and a paranormal investigator will find them self listening hour upon hour from every investigation to very boring sounding audio. You will also easily find yourself falling asleep at times listening to the long audio data or being distracted by other things. Due to this, I want to go over the proper techniques I have learned over the years for effective EVP analysis and gathering.

Once an investigator has done their audio recordings, they then must make the necessary time to sit down and listen to everything carefully. This can be done two different ways, depending on the environment the investigator is trying to do this in. An investigator can analyze first with just a set of headphones or can analyze from a computer with a good loud and clear speaker system. Every investigator wanting to learn good EVP research should have a very good computer with a good audio software program and plenty of hard drive space on the computer. A good investigator will also catalogue and file each audio recording very easily where the recordings can be found easily each and every time for review. There are many very good audio software programs out there to use but I highly recommend Adobe Audition, which I purchased about ten years ago and still highly praise it for any investigator. Due to this, I am going to explain how this audio program can help you as an investigator to find and collect very good EVP's. An investigator should have a good set of headphones (Noise Reduction highly preferred), a good sound card in their computer (like Sound Blaster, etc.), a line in audio patch stereo cable (can be bought at Radio Shack very cheaply for a few dollars), a notebook and pen to take notes, and a good quiet undisturbed private location away from friends and family so that they can listen to all the audio recorded data carefully.

Don't forget to also have an open mind as to what you may be hearing. Make sure you are relaxed and that nothing is bothering you emotionally or physically. In other words, do not do this if you have a headache forming or if many other thoughts are on your mind. It is very good to clear all of your thoughts before sitting down to analyze audio. In other words, don't sit down thinking you are going to get an EVP because the place you investigated looked very spooky and chances are it is haunted because of how the place looked during the investigation.

Keeping an open and clear mind while listening, and taking notes is very important and is effective in not missing anything while you are listening to the recordings. Also make sure that you do not sit and listen for more than 10 to 15 minute increments at a time to ensure that your mind does not wander or where you could possibly fall asleep. Make sure that you are not lying down or in a reclined position while doing the analyzing. Prop yourself up in a good chair with good posture just like you would at your regular job sitting at a computer or desk in the office. Go through the entire audio recording making notes about the times where you think you might have captured something strange, write a brief description of what you thought you heard, make notes about what background noises there are at the time, who was actually present at the time, and then check for any spoken tagging instances before or after the event. Once this is all done properly, you can then move onto the next phase of your audio analyzing.

Once you have effectively written down all your notes about the times on your recording where you think you may have heard an EVP, now it is time to do some heavy duty analyzing on your computer using your audio program software. You need to now plug your digital or analog audio recorder into your computer input or mike line in port and run a recording test on your audio software program to ensure that you can hear your recording properly and loudly enough for analyzing. Once this is done, you then want to go one by one through the recorded sections where you think you might hear a possible EVP. Starting with your first recorded section, you want to record onto your computer about five to ten seconds before and after the actual captured EVP. Once you have been able to record using this method, then loop and playback the recorded section to ensure that you can hear the recording very clearly. Listen to the original recording and try to determine what it is you are hearing.

Next, eliminate all possibilities of naturally occurring sounds. Now, determine if you will need to add any amplification to the original recording to bring it out better. Ask yourself if the recording is loud enough for someone else with an untrained ear to hear what it is you are hearing? Determine again from this what you think the recording is saying and also rule out any possibility of tampering or natural event occurring (example of this is road noise outside, animals outside, etc.). Make your assumption here of what it is you think you are hearing and if you yourself think this is an authentic EVP or not. Also make yourself a note about what you think the EVP is and what questions were being said or asked at the time as to the recorded response you obtained. Make as many personal notes to yourself on the recorded EVP as to you can before moving on to the rest of your recorded audio analysis.

When it comes to EVP analysis research, there are different classes as to EVP's. A person new to this field who has never actually ever obtained an authentic EVP will wonder what the actual EVP recording will sound like. A person will wonder what the dead or spiritual voices actually sound like. A person will find out, surprisingly, that the recorded EVP voices can sound very much like you and me talking, or may sound quite sinister or unearthly sounding. Some EVP recordings can sound very gentle from a child while others may sound very ominous and scary. A person can never truly be prepared by what you may capture on an authentic EVP recording. Some EVP recordings may sound communicative in direct response to an investigator's questions while others will seem to make no sense at all. Some EVP's will sound very clear as if the person is speaking right next to the audio recorder while others will seem to be a mere whisper. Due to this, paranormal researchers have classified authentic EVP recordings into three main types which are simply Class A (very clear sounding, direct, and understandable), Class B (somewhat distorted and not so clear, easy to hear, or understandable), and Class C (very hard to hear, low level, and distant whispering sometimes). Some investigators in this field have even gone a step further and created other deeper levels of classification.

As an experienced paranormal investigator who has obtained hundreds of authentic EVP recordings over the years during my research, I will state that there are no two EVP recordings out there that sound the same to me. Each authentic EVP is unique in its own way due to the circumstances of where and when the EVP was acquired. EVP's can be in a normal speak pattern as a regular person would sound like or they may sound distorted in a faster or slower speak pattern. Some EVP's can even sound metallic, like a robot or non-human is speaking. Some EVP's can also contain just growling or strange noises and have no speaking pattern at all. When it comes to how strange most EVP's sound, I feel that a lot of this is due to the fact that the enteric voices do not have an actual living voice box or larynx like we humans do in controlling how the air travels into our mouths, throat, and over our voice cord a to make a recognizable speech pattern.

What I have also seen and heard is that most authentic EVP's will have a slight vibration effect pattern where they are speaking at either a much higher or lower frequency than the human ear can hear. Many EVP's can also sound quite monotone with no reflection at all in the speech pattern or can sound just like you or me. There are many skeptics out there that I have come across that will try to argue that EVP's are just captured radio broadcasts coming in over certain frequencies. Being experienced, I can undoubtedly state that this is not true at all due to what I have seen and heard and can definitely say that authentic EVP recordings are not miscast radio broadcast frequencies. For certain skeptics it can be point out that in n audio voice recorder, there are no transmitters that can pick up on various anonymous frequencies that travel the air waves like walkie talkies or radios.

When you are able to get your first authentic EVP recording and know the actual conditions that the EVP was captured in, you will easily see how the EVP was captured and the personal situations behind it that make it easy to discern fact from fiction. I have found that the only way to prove this is have a skeptic with you at the time of the investigation and have them see what those actual conditions were from start to finish as to the authentic EVP being gathered. Most of the experienced paranormal investigators in this field do not even care what the skeptics have to say or think because we know from all our years of research about the compelling paranormal evidence we have seen, heard, witnessed, and captured in this field.

A main characteristic of all EVP's is that you will rarely ever hear the same pitch variance in a recorded message or statement. When we hear loved ones however, you will quite easily be able to distinguish the recognized voice of your loved one, family, or relative coming through. It will usually just jump out and knock you on the head, so to speak. When something so extraordinary like this happens to a person, there is total belief at that time that actual communication is taking place and that a certain message is being delivered to them. When quite clear Class A EVP recordings of our loved ones are captured, there is no deniability of what is taking place. One thing that an investigator has to do over time is learn to train your ear to hear EVP's. One may think this is easy to do, but will find that you can easily miss possible EVP's within your recordings if you do not listen correctly.

When an investigator first starts out trying to capture his or her first authentic EVP recording, you are going to have very high expectations as to trying to get a clear Class A EVP. These are of course the easiest to hear of all the classifications of EVP's and the quality, clarity, and loudness of the voice coming through is enough to make you want to do paranormal research for the rest of your life in looking for the answers. It is believed by paranormal researchers that entities making these types of EVP recordings are intelligent, observing, and have learned somehow to manipulate electronic recording mechanisms, transmit, and fine tune the sound waves in such a way that they can actively communicate within this dimension of reality. A way of mental outlook thinking here about Class A EVP's is that it is like the invisible man standing next to you and speaking into your ear even though you cannot see or sense him.

What I have found with Class B EVP recordings is that they are usually not that clear, concise, impressive, but are still authentic EVP's nonetheless. These are usually also EVP's where what is said is not clear enough for another person to hear the same thing that you think is heard. In other words, two or more investigators could easily hear different things being said as to the EVP recording. These EVP's are still very interesting to hear and can still be used as paranormal activity evidence if you have something else to back up or correlate the recording during the investigation. When you obtain and playback a recording such as this to another person, that person may not even hear what it is you are playing for them. An investigator should not get distressed when this happens. Just stand by your notes on what you think it is you have acquired. You will find that the actual audible level of these recordings is usually very low and may sound very distant. The actual meaning may not be understood either and may have nothing to do at all with the actual investigation at the time.

Class B EVP recordings may be intelligent but usually are leaning more towards a possible residual situation where certain sounds or voices are not intelligent and might just be replaying themselves within a certain environment. An example of this might be a distant sounding voice or noise that sounds like a scream, laugh, cry, etc. and could possibly be mistaken for a natural occurring outside noise. This is why tagging during your investigation session is extremely important so that you can later rule out things during your analysis. Due to this, paranormal researchers have quite a bit of difficulty in proving Class B EVP legitimacy to the natural scientific world. This is because scientists trying to prove their theories will always rely on having witnesses to their experiment to prove the reliability and outcome of the experiment.

A scientist also has quite a bit of research backup documentation as to experiment when they present it to the scientific world for acceptance of the theory. In other words, it is quite easy to make a scientific statement about why and how something works, but you must also have the reliable backup data to prove your conclusion about why you think your stated theory substantiates what is actually occurring. If the outcome of the analysis and experiment cannot be agreed upon, then a theory is usually thrown out and not accepted by the scientific community as a whole. This is why paranormal research is so hard to present to the scientific community, because a lot of the time that scientific evidence may not be there due to a supernatural event occurring and the fact that the observers were not there at the time of the experiment, which is usually the case.

Experienced paranormal researchers have to weigh all captured evidence in a limited time and decide what it is can present scientifically and also what evidence has to be discarded due to lack of substantiation. Researchers have a lot of filed information that we personally know is good evidence, but that we cannot for various reasons use at all to prove the existence of paranormal activity.

The final classification of EVP is Class C. These EVP's are very hard to capture, hard to hear, and their overall sound quality is usually very poor. These recordings sound very distorted, faint, and from what I have seen, sound like whispering a lot of the time. Most everyday people new to this field will most often miss these types of EVP's in their recordings because of lack of training, poor hearing, or distraction. Many people might have these types of classifications all over their recordings, but think that they captured nothing at all. It honestly took me almost a year of sincere deep EVP research before I was able to hear and capture these types of EVP recordings. Even a trained experienced paranormal researcher can easily overlook these types of recordings. If you are able to make out even a single word from these types of recordings, you are lucky.

Class C EVP recordings for the experienced paranormal researcher are still interesting, however, in that they might possibly point to the possibility of paranormal activity. With the right type of audio computer software, the experienced paranormal investigator might be able to single out and draw the frequency clearer as to the range that this type of EVP is at. This is also where amplification of the EVP is very important. An investigator can bring up the recording several decibels levels and filter out noise levels to make the recording clearer. It is still very hard for even the experienced investigator to be able to use these types of classification EVP's for possible evidence of paranormal activity. Most of us just find Class C EVP's very interesting from our analysis and then catalogue them into our case files for future reference.

When it comes to the methodology behind effective EVP research, use of the digital audio recorder and possible microphone is one of the best and more direct ways of gathering authentic EVP's. There are other methods you can implore into your

EVP recording sessions. One of these methods utilizes the use of 'white noise'. The definition of white noise according to the *American Heritage Dictionary* is an acoustical or electrical noise of which the intensity is the same at all frequencies within a given band. In other words, the signal contains the same or equal power fluctuation within a fixed bandwidth at a certain center frequency. A more common or visual way of understanding white noise is to think of something you can picture. For example, a steady drip of water from your water faucet into the bathtub would be considered white noise because the water drip is constant a lot of times at a certain sound wave and frequency. Another form of white noise would be when you change to a television or radio station that only has static on it. The modulation of the frequency band is that it is constant and unchanging in its sound audio frequency pattern. The recorded sound of constant flowing ocean waves or flowing air from a fan also could also be considered a form of white noise.

When we go back to our mental thinking in how a disembodied voice could possibly be heard on a taping audio device such as a digital recorder, this is where we need to think more into white noise and its capabilities. Humans have a voice box or larynx that enables us the capacity to speak and make words. Our lips and mouth structure also enable us to be physically able to make and pronunciate words effectively so other people can hear, understand, and communicate back with us. We have to remember here as researchers when we capture EVP's, that the entity forming these words or statements does not have human form, therefore how is it that the entity can form words that are not heard by human ears, but through audio? Could it be that intelligent entities from the other side have figured out how to manipulate electrical recording devices in such a way using frequency fluctuation that they don't need the things that we need to communicate effectively? Are these intelligent, other dimensional beings able to somehow harness the unseen energy around us that we take for granted as to being there and use this energy in such a capacity that they are able to use frequency level modulation to speak and communicate in our recordings?

These are some of the questions that create the drive and passion for paranormal researchers in this field to want to know and learn more about how electronic voice phenomena takes place and how the dead are able to drive their words and meanings across to the dimension of the living so that we are able to hear them. As a person new to paranormal investigation, you will find upon getting your first authentic EVP, that you will soon ask yourself all of these very questions. First you will be amazed at how clear and right there with you your first EVP may sound like, then you will find yourself looking deeper at how that EVP may have occurred and how it is you are able to hear it. This is where white noise comes into play that might better enhance these recordings. In the past, I have used white noise during paranormal investigations. I have found that EVP's happen with the use of white noise and without it. This is where it becomes very intriguing to say the least. With the use of white noise enablers, I have captured EVP recordings which are very clear but sound metallic in nature. This is probably true due to the fact that the voices of the dead or spiritual world are somehow using the set frequency level and pitch of the white noise and manipulating the frequency band in such a way that words and communication are formed. I have found that the use of white noise producers at lower frequency bands seems to work more effectively. It is generally accepted and found that human voices can range from 300 Hz to 1000 Hz. A person will find that many authentic EVP's that are captured either fall under or above this range, but generally at a much lower frequency level. A Hertz (Hz) is measured at one cycle per second. It is found that a dog's hearing frequency range is about 50 to 45,000 Hz while a cat's hearing range is found to be about 45 to 85,000 Hz.

The definition of a decibel according to the *Britannica Concise Encyclopedia* is a unit for measuring the relative intensities of sounds or the relative amounts of acoustic or electric power. Because it requires about a tenfold increase in power for a sound to register twice as loud as loud to the human ear, a logarithmic scale is useful for comparing sound intensity. Thus, the threshold of human hearing (absolute silence) is assigned the value of 0 dB and each increase of 10 dB corresponds to a tenfold increase in intensity and a doubling in loudness. It is found that the human ear can hear sounds that range from 0 dB which are very faint and hard to hear and can vary all the way up to 180 dB which are very loud sounds such as possibly a rocket taking off or a jet engine roaring. Experienced paranormal researchers examine authentic EVP's as waveforms which are the representation of a sound wave (displayed as amplitude against a time constant) and which are characterized as compressed air pressure propagating away from its source of compression. Amplitude is the loudness of a waveform across the peak of the waveform to the trough (the height of waveform). The amplitude is measured in dB on a vertical scale. Researchers also take into consideration the pitch which is the basic frequency by which a certain sound vibrates and how the sound is actually heard, whether high or low, to our ears. Pitch goes hand in hand with the frequency. In other words, the higher the pitch the higher the frequency and so forth.

In understanding how waveforms are created and measured, it allows the paranormal researcher who wants more information on EVP formation, the basics of how sound waves are formed and measured. EVP research again is a very interesting field and it is always very good to have at least one or two people on a paranormal team who can learn more and specialize solely in EVP research methods and who are responsible for gathering any new innovative information that becomes available in this area. These EVP specialists can then train and maintain the rest of the team on effective EVP gathering and analysis protocols.

Another very large area of paranormal research interest right now is in the area of ITC or Instrumental Transcommunication. ITC methods have been around for several years now, but in the past few years there have been some remarkable breakthroughs in ITC experimentation that appear to be breaking the unseen boundaries of communication to the other side. I will explain more about this once I describe to you some ITC devices and methods that are being used a lot more regularly now in paranormal investigation. I am going to explore a few very good ITC methods that have proven them self to be very useful as to capturing possible paranormal activity communication.

Several years ago when I was first getting my "feet wet" in the world of paranormal research, I read several books that described an ITC method where an investigator could use video equipment connected with a television set to produce a captured video ITC method. I must admit that I was very skeptical of this ITC method when I first started to read about it, but at the same time this method really intrigued me. I believe this was due to the fact that sometimes I have actually looked into the static of television sets that I accidently left on late at night after stations went off the air and saw what appeared to be images of some people and places sometimes in the static. This was of course well before the years of cable television where there is non-stop programming on all stations. This was clearly back in the days when television stations would sign off at a very late night and there would be nothing but static on all the television stations at a certain hour of the night. I even remember a time that I thought I heard some words being spoken out of my television late at night which startled and woke me up from a deep sleep.

This video ITC method I am going to describe to you is not easy to do, but it does produce some very interesting video effects that are not ordinary to say the least. This method involves having a video camcorder (any kind will do), a video RCA input line to connect your camcorder to a television, a VCR to connect so that recording can take place, and of course a very clear mind and no distractions whatsoever in the location where you are trying this ITC video experiment. Like I said before, this experiment is not easy to do, but anyone should be capable of hooking everything up correctly with a little know how in how to approach this experiment. First, take your camcorder and either put it on a tripod or rest it on a table surface directly facing your television screen. Then hook your RCA cable input link to your RCA jacks on your television.

At this time, change the channel of your television to where you are able to find a channel with only static on it. Since most televisions are cable hooked these days, all you will need to do is disconnect the cable wire on the back of the television. You should now see complete static on your television. You should also turn down the volume at this time because it can be quite annoying if you are also trying to get some audio for your research. You should leave the volume on a low level. With this camcorder linked to your television, you are creating here what is called a video feedback loop. There is a thought out there among paranormal researchers which is only a theory in that we believe that sometimes feedback loop doorways might exist in electrical devices such as television sets. This again is just pure theory at this time and in no way shape or form is an acceptable scientific approach. I do believe that in the coming years, that this method of ITC will be explored even more deeply than it already is and that there will be some remarkable acceptable breakthrough.

In explaining what feedback loop actually means, it simply means in the world of electronics there is a time when a portion of a circuit's signal is returning to the input point of origin. For example, when we videotape ourselves, we are projecting an image of ourselves on tape. With a feedback loop, the camcorder is actually projecting and taking in the continuous image over and over again, thus creating a feedback loop video signal. When this signal is looked at on the television, it will look very strange and very similar to what warp looks like when a spaceship from Star Trek enters into warp. If you have created the proper feedback loop sequence in hooking up your equipment, you should now see something on your television that looks like you are traveling into an energy tunnel of light

This is the easiest and simplest way to describe what it looks like. Once you get this tunnel effect, you now need to do some adjustments on your camcorder using the zoom function to make the video image closer. When you do this, you will now notice your tunnel effect of lights start to separate from the center of the screen to a wider portion of the television screen towards the corners. You should have a clearer and broader picture at this time. It again is best that you have your camcorder sitting on a tripod when you try this experiment to help prevent the possibility of movement error in the camera and also ensure that you can make adjustments accordingly on the camcorder as to video picture zoom in distance. When you do this, it is better to do this at night where there is hardly any light at all entering the room where you are attempting this experiment. The light on the television will at first seem like a blinding glare, but your eyes should soon become accustomed to it. Keep moving your camcorder so that it is positioned and your lens is adjusted until you see a light effect that will almost seem hypnotizing to the eyes. The right adjustment for this ITC video looping experiment to work should look like a box video screen within a video screen, etc. Again, it will look like you are travelling within an energy tunnel that is very mesmerizing to the eyes. Once you have this set up correctly, then make sure that you have your VCR hooked up with a good tape for recording. Make sure that your VCR connects to your camcorder so that it can pick up what exactly your camcorder is seeing.

Once you feel comfortable with your setup and you feel that you have the right video image on the television which again should be a smaller box area at this time concentrated towards the center of the screen with darkness leading out to the four corners of your television set. Make sure that you can see the smaller box video image clearly with your camcorder. If you feel you have it, then hit record on our VCR and sit back comfortably in a chair observing. Let your VCR record no more than five to ten minute stretches. This is so that you effectively review your video segments frame by frame in slow motion feature on playback. I would recommend that you break up your ITC video direct loop recording sessions into say five sessions for a total of an hour at a time. You now are ready for the playback portion and analysis of what may be on your video tapes.

At this time, go ahead and rewind your tape and make sure you have a notebook and pen in hand to write down the times of when you think you see things in the video and also what it is you think you are seeing. When I say in this instance that you see things, there is a good chance that you may see something, but then again you may have nothing for several sessions. I suggest you do not ever give up and walk away. Do not expect to see something on your very first session. This is what experimentation and conditions are all about when it comes to scientific study. If scientists walked away every time they failed

117

at something, then we would not have the cures for diseases that we have today.

This section is probably the most important step of your ITC video direct look experiment – the analysis. Make sure you are not tired when you review your video taped ITC sessions. It is very important on playback that you do not fast forward or scan your video recordings. If you do, you might miss the images that might have been captured. If you did capture any strange images, they will usually be very short in duration. A person here will ask what is it exactly that I am looking for? A paranormal researcher will be looking for any strange signs of a light anomaly on the television screen image, such as strange colored lights or patterns moving across the screen. Something I did mean to mention is that a person must also be very much in tune with what he or she is doing. In other words, believe in yourself and the fact that you may be able to make contact with the other side. If you don't believe in yourself as to being able to do this effectively, then you are not in the right line of work as far as paranormal research is concerned.

If you think upon looking at your video tapes segments that you possibly see something, then pause the VCR, rewind it, and then playback using a very slow frame advance feature which every VCR has on it. This will allow you to inspect the video image frame by frame in carefully looking at what you think you saw. You will find by doing this, that you will sometimes see images of faces or places in the images. A skeptic will most always state something like these images are just some television station broadcast images that are being captured. Upon closer examination of the video images, a paranormal researcher will see that there are things missing that do not support what a skeptic might theorize.

In the past, I have gotten some video images that I could not explain doing this method. Unfortunately, I had these images on a VCR tape and have moved quite a few times, losing this tape, which was very discouraging to me as an investigator. I learned early on that every investigator must take all necessary steps to preserve each and every piece of paranormal evidence that is acquired. I must admit that I have not done this method for a few years or as much as I wanted to in the past, but this is because I tend to really be more focused as an investigator in the EVP research area. This is not to say that any area of research is more important or exciting than another, but every investigator will go off on a certain path of new research discovery in this field.

When you capture strange video images doing the ITC direct feed loopback video experiment, you will see that the faces that sometimes appear are usually always by themselves. There is never more than one face in the picture at the same time. It almost always appears that the image might look as if it is reaching out to you or looking, as if the imaged face can really see you. This may sound a quite bit creepy to most people, but it is the truth about what this method will provide. When you see your first image utilizing this method, you will literally feel your skin crawl. This is a natural physical and mental reaction to seeing something like this. I have seen upon looking at the images, that the heads sometimes appear to be turned towards the subject as if trying to say something. I must admit that I have only gotten just a few video images in the past using this experimentation method, but that I was truly very astonished by the results.

When you are able to try this experiment, if you are able to capture anything strange, you will also be very surprised at your findings. Again, I must point out that the chances of getting something here are only at a very minimal percentage. Skeptics to this method will again try to claim over and over that these images are just fragments of broadcast from television stations, but an investigator or the sensible person can quite easily see that this is not the case when these images are captured. This is the same thinking when authentic EVP's are captured. If you decide to take an interest in exploring more into ITC direct feed loopback video experimentation methods, I highly encourage experimentation in this area of research. There are many researchers right now exploring in different ITC areas, but I have not seen a whole lot of experimentation coming out of this particular area presently. Who knows, you may be the first to really catch onto something and become the next major pioneer in this area of ITC research.

The next area of experimentation and research that I am going to discuss are previously discussed electrical device methods of ITC. I wanted to discuss this particular method because of how interesting I found it when I actually found out more about it and tried the session for the first time. Many people have seen this method described as being used by Nostradamus and other prophets from the past. One in hearing all the stories and prophecies of Nostradamus and others will wonder how exactly they were able to see the future and make the predictions that were made and how some of these prophecies appear to have come true over the ages. This way of viewing things has been called scrying and appears to again have been used by many ancient cultures as a prediction indicator for seeing the future, speaking with the spirits of the dead, and in some cases, even used in a form of remote viewing later said to have been used even in the Central Intelligence Agency.

When I first found out about the process of Scrying, I had read about this subject in several books. I also saw this method used in several movies and especially one in particular, *Constantine*. When seeing these types of things in the movies, the public usually and generally almost always characterizes these practices as either being taboo or make believe. Initially a person would look at this subject as being something magical, but I soon found that it appeared to work. I had read several books on the subject beforehand and had a genuine interest as to exploring more into this ancient method. I want to also state here quite simply that this method has nothing to do with the practice of Witchcraft or even the dark ritual arts as they are described by some.

Let me first describe more what actual scrying is. It is a method that is used as a tool to open the senses or your possible psychic self, so that you can project an astral image from your sub-conscious self to your conscious self. This is used by many sensitive people in this field of research in order to be able to see what we are called auras. In the paranormal field, auras are energy that is radiated supposedly from each of us even though we do not knowingly see it. It is believed by some to be the actual radiance from our own soul energy. Auras can with most people be a different color. I have actually seen images taken through methods of Kirlian photography which show the electrical energy left by different objects and human's where an energy form or shape is left behind, in some cases, the actual aura of a person.

Kirlian photography involves a high voltage field creating an image on film when the actual picture is taken. When a subject's body temperature and energy field fluctuates, pictures are taken. There is a way to hook a sensor to the actual camera that can transform a subject's actual electromagnetic radiated field into certain vibrating frequencies that are then captured and simulated to show certain colors that are created, thus showing the aura changes in a person. This method of photography is much more easily explained by doing internet searches on it and then looking at the actual pictures that are created.

Going back to the ancient method of scrying , this all ties together in a sense as to what so called ancient seers or prophets used as to possibly viewing the future. One of these is the very famous Nostradamus who used scrying methods to prophesize certain revelations of future events that many have claimed to have come true as to what he had previously seen. It involves many things as to being able to do this, but mainly a person has to be very relaxed. When I first read and started to research scrying, I have to admit that I was a skeptic because I had tried it a few times in the beginning with no results happening for me. I was beginning to give up on it and throw it out as a possible hoax method when I soon realized that I was not doing it right and I was not nearly relaxed as I should have been with my conscious self and that there were always outside distractions which affected the scrying sessions that I had tried to complete.

Now, before I further describe what actually needs to be done here, I want to make quite sure that you understand that I am being very sane and rational here as to describing how to do this and what I did experience doing this method. I have to admit that it was quite scary at times when I did it, and that I have only done it approximately six or seven times trying to get the full sensation of it occurring. I have only attempted to do it this many times because of the feeling that I had of losing control and drifting away. I will explain to you in a moment what is meant by this when I describe this floating away or losing control feeling that I experienced. When I felt it, it was quite unnerving to say the least and that I did not expect to feel what I had felt previously. I again am a very experienced paranormal investigator and am also in a sense a skeptic of something new till I am able to lay witness to it actually working. In other words, I will not recommend or talk about something of this nature if I do not believe that it works.

When society thinks of scrying for those who actually know what it means, many people will refer to this as a method of looking or gazing into the crystal ball, and for the sake of things, most people associate crystal balls with being able to see into the future, supposedly, or see visions of certain things both past and possibly present. It all is really the same thing in a certain sense of logic as to these methods and their association towards scrying. It all essentially is the same thing. Scrying can be associated to date back approximately four to five thousand years ago and is sometimes said to originate from the Sumerian culture. This was a very advanced culture of people at that time that appeared very advanced and also appeared to be considered the sudden civilization. Much of this information was discovered from ancient Sumerian scribes that were found that depicted a very advanced and educated culture of people that appeared suddenly. This ancient civilization was considered to also be the first humans to create their first form of known language, literature, and writings as well as forms of advanced science that included mathematics, theology, botany, zoology, biology, etc. The question for many is who were these people and where exactly where did they originate from so quickly while forming civilizations in comparison to our own existence. These people appeared to be highly advanced and the question for many is where they got all of this knowledge. This is of course is enough information for another book as to the ultimate question. Again scrying methods appeared to have originated from their culture many thousands of years ago.

Scrying again relies on and is very important as to the manipulation of your self conscious as to being able to mentally focus and clear your mind of any distractions. This does take practice at a few attempts to make sure you are doing what is necessary to relax and focus your energy and thinking in the right direction in attaining the results necessary. This again, I want to reassure you, has nothing to do with associating one's self with any dark arts or anything. This again is just a method of being able to see without the necessary use of your eyes by opening up the facilities of the human mind. The human brain has been known to have several areas of it that are not even used by us for everyday tasks and it is believed that as we grow older from being children and your adolescents, that certain parts of our mind are simply closed off due to the thinking that society invokes on us the way we should be thinking. I know this sounds strange but it is true. We are in a sense made to block off areas of our human mind and its capability as we grow older in the ways that we learn and educate ourselves. We again are made to believe through logic that monsters and sinister things that lurk in the dark are highly perceived to be fictitious and non-existing. This makes us all question what exactly are monsters of the dark? Are the vampires, werewolves and other things that are commonly shown to us by means of televised and written media or are the so called monsters of the dark something much more sinister, scary, and horrifying than even our known senses can imagine? Could the human mind be such a much more powerful tool and have much more use, possibly seeing into other worlds or dimensions that co-exist along with our own?

In looking at ancient cultures and even our own modern world, many cultures always had a certain religious belief that gods were present and not far away where we could reach out to them. Gods were always portrayed in ancient writings as existing high up on a mountain or down within the deep confines of earth or in our own modern religious sense of the words heaven or hell. Scrying again was originally created as a sense of being able to communicate with the dead initially and see past the barriers of what our senses perceive in the physical world around us. There again for this method are varying types of tools that a person can use. For the sake of modern use, I am going to explain the use of a mirror because the mirror has always been explained through folklore and other means to possess a quality of allowing one to be able to see to the other side or other dimension besides our own. Mirrors have always fascinated people and some people actually are afraid to have mirrors in their homes for this fact.

People in the early 1700's in areas such as Louisiana believed that when someone was very close to death, that all the mirrors in the house had to be covered and then taken out of the house and replaced once the person actually died. It was believed that if a mirror was not covered when a person died, that their soul or spirit would travel into the mirrored dimension and become trapped for eternity because the spirit would be misguided. This story may not be believed by everyone, but it was taken very serious by people of the time. I have traveled through Louisiana and some of the plantations there and was told that this superstition was very prevalent and believed during those older times.

To accomplish this method of paranormal communication, a person would need what is called black mirror or a mirror with a black backing. This simply could be a piece of glass that is painted one side several times with black paint or you may be able to simply purchase a mirror in the store with a sealed black face to it. To begin this method, you will again need a good area. This should be a very quiet and dim lighted area, such as possibly a closet, back bathroom, or something. You will also need to make sure that you cannot see your dim light source at all in the actual mirror. With the actual focal point of where you are looking into the mirror as to where you placed it, you should not be able to see the light source at all. You could possibly try a small light flashlight or candle for this experiment. Make sure that this light source is positioned low and behind where you are sitting. Now, once seated, you must practice making yourself relaxed. Again, if you have family or other people in the immediate area, this would probably be better to do when you are completely alone.

While taking your breaths, look into the darkness in front of you and start to relax yourself. The mirror should again be put on a counter, your lap, or something in front of you at a good enough angle where you cannot see your reflection in it or anything at all. There should be a sense of a glow in the mirror from your low light source but nothing else. Allow your focus once you are relaxed to fall down onto the mirror. You should have previously tilted your mirror approximately forty-five degrees at an angle away from your direct viewing access. In other words, have the mirror facing somewhat in your focal point, but also at an angle away from you. If on a counter top, put something under the mirror so that you can accomplish this angle of viewing it. Once you have relaxed and focused on the placed mirror, then start to let your mind drift where you are not thinking about anything. You should also not have any thoughts of trying to forcefully make this work. You must remember that you are trying to awaken your internal abilities as to using the other areas of your mind. Your gaze on the mirror should be so relaxed and your head positioned comfortably in such a way that you have no trouble keeping your fixation on the mirror in front of you.

If you are relaxed enough and have everything set in such a way, you should start after approximate five to ten minutes start to feel something different. I again can tell you that I had read about this and tried it a few times with nothing happening. I soon learned that I was too anxious and not calmed down enough when I had tried those earlier sessions. I was not seeing anything after several minutes of those previous sessions and was starting to believe that everything I had read about on this subject was not true. It was approximately the seventh session trying this that things started to change and I saw the reality of this. If you are doing this the right way, after a few minutes of relaxation, and a fixed gaze upon the mirror, you should then sense your fixed vision to take

126

on blurry change and a heavy feeling like you are going to sleep. It to me actually feels the same as to when you are watching television very late at night and really want to stay awake to watch something, but for some reason you fall asleep a few minutes and then come to not remembering ever falling asleep. This is the same feeling you will feel with this method, but when you feel it, you must do everything in your power not to close your eyes or let yourself go to sleep. Ignore these feelings for approximate a minute of feeling them, and they will go away all of a sudden and you will then feel very awake. You will find that all of a sudden you have a sort of tunnel vision sensation of staring at the mirror and being pulled into the mirror. When I first sensed this feeling of being pulled, I jerked and unfortunately brought myself out of the session. I really hated this because I felt that something was really about to happen and it was a very strange feeling. If you close your eyes for any reason during this method, you will also come right out of it, so do everything you can to keep your eyes open and focused intently on the mirror in front of you. By keeping your eyes open, you will start to feel this pulling sensation and also feel a side to side sensation as if your head is moving even though it is not. Your head will become very heavy for a few moments and then get very light. It is at this moment that spectacular things should begin to unfold in the mirror in front of you.

While you were doing all of this, the mirror in front of you should have looked a little opaque with a light source barely lighting it. You again if placed right at the appropriate angle, should only have been able to see a very dim glow in the mirror. This should have been somewhat dark, but at the same time visible to your eyes up to this point. Your field of vision at this time should see what looks like a picture starting to form in the mirror and a certain glow starts to appear in the mirror. This glow becomes brighter and brighter to you. This will seem very startling to you when you first see it and you will have the urge to jerk or look away because of how unbelievable this event will seem that is unfolding in front of you. Once the glow occurs and builds up, it will then start to fade into a normal lighted picture. You should then begin to see what looks like mist or clouds forming and moving across the image. Some people I have talked to about this have seen other things like twinkling lights, sparks, or other things. Most people however that have tried this successfully usually see the mist forming moving cloud sensation. Certain images of things will then suddenly pop into the picture. These images should appear very vivid and quite strange; they will usually consist of people or locations. Usually people or locations you have no idea as to who or where they are. Very seldom do people see things that are familiar to them.

By trying this method, many believe that they can communicate with their loved ones through either sight or sound. This is accomplished by the same method described but this time you will be using a picture of the loved one you are trying to communicate with. You can also use an object that the person used to own that was cherished by them. You can hold this object in your hands while you try the same scrying method. This time, however, you will change things up just a little. This time have the picture of your loved one directly sitting in front of you. Have your scrying tool mirror either to the left or right of the mirror approximately six to ten inches. While you do the same method, concentrate you fixed focus gaze on the picture this time. As you relax deeply, state the name of the loved one out loud and that you are trying to reach them. Keep your gaze on the features of your loved one and look into their eyes. Keep doing this until the same glow starts to appear and the mist or cloud sensation starts to form. Then slowly take your gaze from the picture to the positioned mirror. Think about the person whom you are trying to communicate with as you view into the mirror. State the name of the loved one or person you are trying to reach in a soft low whisper several times in a similar fashion. You should see the same glow appear again in the mirror and once it subsides gradually, you should then see the face of your loved one in the mirror.

The strange thing that you will see is that this image of your loved one moves, changes facial expression, and might possibly talk to you. You will see the lips move but hear the words in your head quite clearly. It is at this time that you can ask those questions in a low voice but give them time to answer you back. Sometimes this might go on for several minutes and might appear to be a dreamlike state, but in reality you will realize that you are quite awake and experiencing this. It is quite amazing to a person who tries this the right way and succeeds doing it. This also again in no ways is considered dangerous or invoking something dark in our lives. It is just a tool that is used as a way of communicating mentally and visually to the other side. There will be skeptics who might laugh at you when you describe your successful experience and this will be hard because you will personally know the reality of what you just experienced.

If this occurs, just keep it to yourself and know that this did occur. I again was very skeptical when I first did this with nothing at all occurring for several tries. Once I succeeded, I was able to see the face of someone I knew and loved. I have never told anyone in my family about this up to now because they might not have believed me at the time. It was my deceased favorite uncle who had passed away several years prior and I was not able to make it for his funeral and felt very guilty for that because my ex-wife had gotten the message as to this and had forgotten to tell me in time for me to make the trip for his funeral. He had a stroke and had passed away suddenly in his sleep one day. He had smiled to me that day and told me that it was alright, he was in a good place and watching from there.

Now, I could literally talk about this area of paranormal research for something like eons, but I will cut you a break and assume here from my words in this chapter that you have a good enough understanding as to methods and communication I have mentioned and described in relation with who we as researchers are trying to contact and label in our terminology as the dead. The real question in our communication is they really the dead? I personally tend to think of death or our passing as only a modest simple word and possibly the actual beginning of our ultimate learning experience and existence. They say that ultimate wisdom is based on ultimate knowledge. Could this be what we take with us as to our consciousness carrying on even after the death of our physical bodies? These are so many questions that we as paranormal researchers ask ourselves in our quests as to seeking the paranormal truths that very possibly do exist out there.

# Chapter 7: Paranormal Discussion – What Are Ghosts??

Now, we know that we all do paranormal investigations in order to find and confirm the existence of ghosts. The questions that we need to ask ourselves in the first place are why we are trying to find ghosts, and what ghosts actually are? They are something unknown that exists within our physical plane of reality the way that we know it. I point this out because if we do not all have a better understanding of what it is that we are seeking, then how can we all be good paranormal investigators and researchers, using our personal methods of trying to find good scientific factual evidence and proof of ghosts.

In coming up with better solutions in all our methods for great paranormal investigation and getting the verifiable evidence for proof, the first question we all should be asking ourselves personally is exactly how do we define ghosts? We have to review any credible paranormal evidence (video, audio, scientific instruments) that we have gathered and that is already out there for us to see. If we know better what it is that we are trying to investigate and what kind of evidence we are looking for, than chances are our correlated evidence will be a lot more credible if our paranormal investigative research is backed up from more than one source. There are many definitions out there by people, and this term ghost is rather broad as to its overall meaning. A common simple definition used by many paranormal investigators out there is that a ghost is the actual physical manifestation or spirit of a person or animal that used to be living at some time but is now dead.

I do tend to believe this but the paranormal world also involves some other things out there that many of us tend to believe were not living at any one

questions that I asked myself at a young age when I read nearly every book on the paranormal and ghosts that I could find. I then started out on my own paranormal quest for the answers.

When paranormal investigators think of ghosts, we all think of something unseen, maybe appearing and registering in some sort of an energy manifestation whether that is an actual apparition composition of sorts. It is a very clear understandable EVP disembodied voice or sound, a sudden very unexplainable drop or increase in temperature for no apparent reason, a feeling of extreme static energy discharge on our skins that feels like we are being touched, and in the most extreme paranormal cases, things being moved or thrown. Sometimes there are actual people being attacked in some manner physically by some unseen force or entity. When these types of things occur for paranormal investigators for which there is no explainable natural reasoning present, than we characterize this as a paranormal activity or an event where either a ghost or ghosts are present.

It is from this vantage point as serious paranormal investigators/researchers that we should take the broad definition of what a ghost is a little further here. If we take this material thinking a little deeper at how we can further approach good paranormal investigations, than chances are that we will discover and invent newer methodology and investigation practices along the way and also find and use better reliable scientific equipment means in determining why ghosts are here and how they actually physically manifest themselves to us. If we all as investigators/researchers take this mental stance to exploring a lot deeper instead of just seeing if there are possible ghosts in a possible haunted environment, then chances are that we will all over time contribute a lot more credible paranormal evidence about what ghosts consist of, why they appear the ways they do to us, how they are able to communicate with us, and so forth. An example here would be if you personally were to explore the history of paranormal investigation/research up to this present time. You will see that there were several pioneers to this research field and that they all contributed something to better help this research field along and assist with our understanding of ghosts and the greater possibility that they are not a myth and do actually exist right in front of our eyes, although unseen as a matter of perspective. The major question for each of you reading this to consider is how deep into the paranormal world of ghosts do you personally want to go? Is this just a simple hobby for you to see if you can find something that may resemble something ghostly or are you looking for even deeper researched theories and answers to what ghosts are and why they are here?

Now, for any average person to want to take paranormal ghost research to a much higher level than just simple ghost hunting, that person would have to ask themselves what they are hoping to gain from this. That person will also have to examine themselves about their degree of skepticism towards the existence of ghosts. In other words, don't just believe in the existence because of what other paranormal investigators are telling you they experienced or from what you possibly saw on television in a paranormal show. Go outside, see, and experience it for yourself as a good investigator.

I will address some overall skepticism towards this research field in my next chapter a lot more, but wanted to state here that this is an attitude that most people have to get around to have a much deeper appreciation towards this research field for what it presents to us. Myself and every other really good paranormal investigator/researcher out there after years of doing this approaches every paranormal investigation case with a certain degree of being objective to the known information at hand, but we do not offer our overall investigator paranormal opinion until there has been a thorough review of credible paranormal activity and evidence from more than one controlled correlated instrument source. In other words, we do not just offer our professional opinion on what others have said, or if we only acquired some possible paranormal evidence from one source and it was not correlated with other devices. I'm sorry, but a spike on a K2 EMF meter by itself does not constitute paranormal activity and that a ghost is present in an environment. A good paranormal investigation leader always examines and openly discusses with their team entirely all the parameters of the pre-investigation and investigation results.

If we as good investigators start looking at the different types of collected data and experiences we are all having a lot closer, then we can determine better correlated reliable scientific instruments to use in conjunction with each other and will be able to confirm what ghosts may be composed of and how it is they can materialize in certain ways. We also all need to learn in protocol fashion how to investigate better and how to set up controlled location environments with several paranormal equipment devices for correlation. Maybe we can determine better ways to see evidence on video and capture direct communication on audio from ghosts in conversation. We as investigators have always thought how neat it would be to sit down and have a good discussion, to see what that ghost/spirit might tell us. It sounds funny in the thought, but these are the types of things that researchers are striving for each and every day.

For most of us, we already know that ghosts exist from everything we have seen and experienced over the years; the big question for us is how can we get better evidence to prove scientifically to the rest of the world that without any doubt, ghosts are real and do exist? I will tell you what I personally believe a ghost is. A ghost to me is a big confirmed enigma that I am going to research till the day that I die, and that I believe and predict that all my gathered research and that the research of other serious paranormal researchers in this field will yield to the scientific world, astonishing and compelling scientific evidence proof in the next 25 years that ghosts are real. Great paranormal researchers get closer and closer to this goal with more sophisticated equipment each and every day, that day of scientific realization about this research field is coming.

# Chapter 8: Paranormal Skepticism

I just had to cover this discussion topic in a book such as this. There are many reasons that this area has to be discussed. Upon the release of any good paranormal research book on ghosts, there is always going to be a certain degree of public and media interviews and also possible strong outside the box skepticism towards this topic. I have actually seen this already through the media before because I have done news station and radio station paranormal interviews before where they will contact me usually around Halloween time and tell you that they are looking for a good story on ghosts and the paranormal haunted world. I do find it funny that the general media only really appears to take notice of the paranormal world of ghosts around the October time frame when in fact the paranormal is very interesting as a topic, and paranormal activity occurs at all times of year all around us with no specific time frame. It seems to me that some of these stations are just trying to create a hot topic to discuss for ratings sake at that time of year. I actually have never seen or witnessed paranormal activity increase more just because any given paranormal investigation was conducted on October 31st.

What I personally found upon being interviewed by either news or radio stations is that they would appear very interested initially in getting a person to come in and do either a live or recorded segment with them on the air. They would start off acting like they really believe in ghosts, but at the same time would shy away at some point of the interview when asking questions and take a rather skeptical point of view towards ghosts. This does not always occur, because there is good television news and radio media people out there who have a sincere interest and really do believe in the paranormal and ghosts and want to show the public world the good evidence just like we do. The other thing that I always found somewhat difficult with doing some media interviews, would be that they would put you either on video or audio tape where they will ask what appear to be good paranormal questions and a person usually answers these questions one by one honestly and intelligently thinking that they will air it as such, this is usually in pre-recorded instances and not live obviously. A person will then wonder what the news or radio interview segment will sound like once edited. Everyone must realize that editing will always take place no matter what because of length of air time that they can show the video segment or play the audio segment. Once that segment is aired, that person will either be relieved or shocked by what they hear.

Sometimes a news station will change things that you state about ghosts and the paranormal and edit it according to what they think their audiences want to hear. This does not always occur, but when it does, it is mildly upsetting because the media will then air that degree of skepticism towards ghosts in general and make you sound like you believe in ghosts but on the other hand that you may be skeptical of what you find. I had this occur once, and my interview seemed strange. I did not object to the interview footage, but I could see how they were trying to do a story element as to both sides of the fence, from believing ghosts to a skeptical point of view that maybe ghosts did not exist. This is two sides of the forum or arena so to speak. I have seen great news and radio paranormal segments where everything went off just great without a hitch. The news station video interview segments that I really like to see are the ones where the station is interested enough to come along for the paranormal investigation themselves and see what it is that the investigators find and how they do everything. The news reporters and camera people in those instances usually encounter their own personal paranormal experiences to remember and discuss on tape from their perspectives.

The other kind of person that is encountered at times in the paranormal investigation field is what can be labeled as the extreme skeptic or a hater of the paranormal. This is usually a person that no matter what you can say or show them as to great paranormal evidence, they will simply not believe you and discredits the information and labels it hogwash. They will usually be rather aggressive in their actions to discredit everything the paranormal world has offered and presented as credible evidence. They will tell you to your face that it all is just a big put on to gain attention or money for other purposes. Now, for the serious paranormal investigator, this can be quite insulting and it is really easy to become angry and vocal over this. A lot of verbal arguments or spats will usually take place over this but the seasoned experienced paranormal investigators out there including me have all encountered this thinking during the years and we all have learned to simply ignore and walk away from it. We have learned that everyone out there has their own thinking on certain things, and that there really is nothing that a person can say to a skeptic to persuade a change in that, especially on the topic of ghosts. Why waste all of our energy and time as good investigators in trying to do combat with someone we know will not change no matter what we say or present to them? We should save all that energy for what we do, investigate ghosts. Ignore and run away from the skeptics. Who really cares what they think anyway?

If we all look at our personal roots and why we all took interest and entered the paranormal research field in the first place, then we will see that it does not matter what other people might think, but rather what new things we keep discovering about ghosts. What I have seen over the years is a big increase in people who do believe without a doubt that ghosts do exist and are reality. I don't know if this sudden change is because people are suddenly experiencing strong personal unexplainable ghostly encounters or if this belief is coming from the paranormal investigation television shows that show pretty good paranormal evidence firsthand for the world to see and make judgment on. There has also been talk of some paranormal investigation television shows intentionally faking or making up paranormal evidence for the purpose of gaining more ratings.

Now, I will never actually accuse someone directly or indirectly in this fashion of intentionally faking paranormal evidence unless I witness and can prove it. Just the mere fact that someone is telling or showing me that this is taking place is not good enough for me to make that conclusion or observation. I would hope that others in the paranormal research field are the same way. In other words, don't just join that posse out there that is out to get someone just because they are telling you that they have acquired evidence. See for yourself and make your own objective observations about what is being presented. There are always two sides to every story out there. I do see that this talk about paranormal evidence being faked on television does somewhat hurt and discredit the really good paranormal evidence that is found by other serious investigators in this field like myself and my team.

One thing that I find strange is that there are some paranormal investigation groups in the paranormal television world and also the public out there who state that they are extremely skeptical of the paranormal world and they seem to only be in this paranormal field to debunk the belief in ghosts. Out of professional respect, I am not going to name who these groups are, but most of the paranormal world probably already has an idea of who I am discussing here because their actions over the years have been quite blatant and intrusive to the paranormal field in general. Now, I find that very ironic. Why would any paranormal investigator on any paranormal television show or regular common every day paranormal team come into the paranormal investigation world just to try to debunk everything they can find? That does not prove anything scientifically and only hurts this field. Aren't we all in this field because of our passion, love, desire, and curiosity as to seeing what else we can discover and prove as to ghosts? Sure, every paranormal investigator has to have some slight degree of skepticism or else that person would not be a good investigator, but to approach this field with animosity towards trying to debunk everything that is witnessed as to the paranormal, those people in my opinion should not even be in this field at all. They are only hurting it for the rest of us.

I can agree with some of the level of skepticism that some possess about the paranormal world of ghosts. Without this skepticism, there would be no good questions that are asked and no intelligence or findings discovered. There also would not be a drive for all of us to get better each and every day at our practice in paranormal research. There has to be some control line in any experimentation that we do in this field. It is like being in a laboratory working on trying to develop something, whether that is a chemical that is used in our household, or something that is created for medicinal purposes, etc. When all experimentation is done, several tests have to be run in determining if what is discovered is correct and can be backed up by additional formulated data. There has to be a certain degree of quality control in any laboratory analysis that is conducted. This control element enables paranormal investigators in environments to further isolate any controlled possible evidence that is found in order to detect and correct any present deficiencies in the methods that we used in gathering that paranormal data. If the proper finely detailed quality control methods and observations are used each and every time the same way during a controlled paranormal investigation, then the results and great paranormal evidence that is found will be better correlated and explainable from a scientific viewpoint and backed up through theory and conclusion. I will better explain some paranormal theories in an upcoming chapter, but for now want to address this for the purposes of some skeptics out there.

There will always be skeptics and non-believers to the paranormal research field about the existence of ghosts. This is because the world is full of skeptics in just about anything. Skeptics exist for one sole purpose, and that is so they can gain more power at being skeptical. For some, this is the way they think and the way they were programmed as they grew up. Some were made at a very young age to not believe in anything that is presented about ghosts possibly existing. Some were told within their religion that it is against the Bible to believe in such a thing as ghosts. Some are just pessimistic towards many things in their lives to not believe. You know what? It's okay to have skeptics in this field of paranormal research. Again, without skeptics, paranormal investigators would not be challenged to find those better methods of investigation and discover those theories that might prove what it is that we believe in, which are ghosts. I have seen that for every skeptical person that exists in this world that does not believe that ghosts exist, there is another hundred people out there who do believe. It seems that public opinion number is increasing more and more each day as people are experiencing the paranormal world of ghosts more. More people are now coming out and stating that maybe those very strange experiences and encounters that they personally had over the years. Maybe, just maybe that was actually paranormal in nature. They are starting to believe that those things that are seen by people out of the corners of their vision, fast moving fleeting shadows, that maybe those are very real. That those noises that are heard late into the night as to footsteps and things moving about, maybe that could possibly be a ghost lurking around unseen. In that instance when you felt something crawl up and move about on your bed while you were sleeping, could have possibly been something paranormal in nature. These are all rhetorical questions normal human beings ask ourselves each and every day as to the paranormal world of ghosts, that they possibly do exist and that we are very sane as to believing in their existence.

I again do not personally try to make other people believe in the existence of ghosts. I as an investigator actually get the evidence to show them firsthand that ghosts exist. This is not just some hobby to me; it again is very serious research work. I tend to believe that the only way for another person to draw their conclusions as to ghosts is to take that person into that environment and have them see for themselves. The only way for any skeptical person to believe in something that seems so mentally distant to them as the possibilities of ghosts existing, is have that person to experience it. I am not afraid of people offering their skepticism of this paranormal world of ghosts. I welcome it.

I tend to find 3 things that might be the reasons that people are skeptical of ghosts: 1) They are just not open minded enough to the possibility. 2) Their religion and religious beliefs in some fashion puts them on guard as to believing in anything having to do with the paranormal world. 3) They might be afraid of certain possibilities that something unseen might exist right in front of their own eyes watching them. 4) They might just be the type of person that just likes to be ignorant so that they can be different and hold some power over others such as being skeptical of most things. These are all observations that I have made on skeptics and ghosts. Again, it is okay to be skeptical as long as they as skeptics don't try to persuade me to think otherwise. You see, I know that ghosts exist. I have witnessed and experienced them many times over the years. No skeptical person out there is going to make me believe otherwise and I would hope that this carries true to your thinking and interest also.

# Chapter 9: Paranormal Theories

I want to warn with a big flashing light that some of you will find this chapter very interesting, some of you may get a little bored, and some of you may just fall asleep. All in all, this chapter should be enjoyable and I will hinge onto several talked about paranormal theories out there and also some theories of my own.

When we think of the word theory and its meaning, let us first define what a theory actually is for anyone out there who may not already know this from scientific jargon. According to the *Merriam-Webster Dictionary online*, it states that a theory can be 3 things: 1) the analysis of a set of facts in their relation to one another. 2) A plausible or scientifically acceptable scientific procedure or body of principles offered to explain phenomena. 3) A hypothesis assumed for the sake of argument or investigation. These definitions pretty much clearly state what a theory is. Now that I have gotten the definitions of the word out of the way, let us move on to discussing theory and some of its applications to the paranormal research world.

In the theories that lie within the paranormal world, there are many that are floating out there, but only a few that seem to pop up over and over again quite a lot in discussion. These theories were derived as possible explanations to what may be occurring in different phenomenon and are encountered by paranormal researchers over time in this field. Some of these theories seem very understandable and plausible while some others may seem, well, way out there in space. I will do my best here to make the more complex theories a little more understandable for you. I have noticed that some good paranormal researchers who have written books on this topic are actual scientists in certain fields of study and it appears that they may have forgotten that some people out there may not necessarily understand their jargon that is used in their books. Some theories out there may be deep in certain perspective.

One of the common theories out there about ghosts and spirits is that they may enter or leave through something known as a portal. This portal or doorway in a lot of perspectives is seen as a point where two possible dimensions intersect each other in some sort of fashion. Very much like the portal we all grew up seeing in the movie Poltergeist in that famous closet scene. These portals however in the real modern paranormal research world are not all lit up, glowing, or flashing like a strobe in the movies. In fact, these portals in a lot of real instances are hidden, invisible, and in many cases, hard to find or prove. Sometimes these portals may be an area on a wall, on the floor, the ceiling, or even suspended in mid-air where either the temperature does not feel the same at all, or there is a degree of unseen strange energy felt there, as in a peculiar disturbance whether that be electrical or ionic in nature. It is hard to describe unless you actually encounter a portal on your own. When I say temperature difference, I mean a really different ambient temperature from the overall temperature in an environment. It is either very warm or very cold in respect to every other area in that environment with no possible rational explanation for that difference of temperature or electrical disturbance being there.

When we as paranormal investigators put our electro-magnetic meter devices into these areas, the meters literally go crazy off the scale in their readings. Remember from previous discussion that if you are a good investigator, you would have already done all your baseline readings of that investigated environment so you already know where all the naturally occurring electro-magnetic fields are and what their normal ranges show.

Some will say that these portals are also fixed and do not move from those certain areas, almost as if they are already mapped out in our dimension. We just don't know it. Think for instance over a period of two hundred years in a certain location and all the changes that may have taken place on that land over that two hundred year period. You may see several structures come and go, but that portal may remain over time in exactly the same place. We, as paranormal researchers know that this sounds strange, but we also believe this portal explanation to be very plausible from all of our experiences and encounters about exploring the paranormal world. A lot of people will argue and say that Ouija boards are very dangerous because they can open a portal to the other side where anything can enter: ghosts, spirits, demons, or who knows what else. Maybe even extraterrestrials enter through these portals from another dimensional universe very different from our own.

It is hard to say exactly why these portals are there, but we do know one thing, that the possibilities are there that these portals truly exist for some reason. Some out there think that these portals have to do with the natural ley lines in relation to the earth's magnetic fields. Ley lines have to do with intersecting points of interest or actual monuments like Stonehenge that were put their possibly for spiritual psychic or mystical purposes. These ley lines actually run all over the place and over time, it can be seen that a lot of structures are built right on top of these lines without people even knowing it. On the topic of Ouija boards, I can accept the arguments that people make as to the possibilities of them opening portals because of past paranormal cases I have done. In those cases, there did always appear to be a portal somewhere in the location and a Ouija board always seemed to be associated with when the paranormal activity first began. It is my belief that people sometimes do things with Ouija boards that they should not as in daring spirits/ghosts to do things or by simply playing around thinking that it all is a game. The use of a Ouija board or any device as a matter of fact in trying to contact the other side is definitely not a game and should be taken seriously by people. I have seen very bad things occur to people when they were not responsible as to using a Ouija board. For the most part, I personally believe that people should stay away from Ouija boards. I have encountered too many bad cases where people did not. In those cases, it did appear that a portal was opened and that dark dangerous entities did enter those people's lives and wreak havoc as a result.

There are some researchers that believe that these portals again are fixed and that they may open and close on their own over time for various reasons. Some of these portals may remain open on a constant basis. When we think of portals, a good way of picturing this concept would be to think of the movie *Stargate*. In that movie, there is a portal that goes into a state of flux or shifting in and out in entirely different universes or dimensions interacting with each other. That of course is just a movie, but the concept they rely upon comes from paranormal foundations. Paranormal portals are believed to act very similar to this. From the few portals that I have actually witnessed, they appear to be that of a mist forming in mid-air out of nothing and then going into some sort of rotation pattern. The mist usually is not well defined at all, but can be seen by the naked eye when it forms, even in extreme darkness. In the past, I have tried to take pictures or even take video of these phenomena when they occur, but nothing ever comes out on the video camcorder or camera.

When it comes to portals, it is believed that they only allow a partial flow of whatever is coming through, but sometimes they may allow the whole of something unseen. This may be for some of the reasons that we are not able to see when this actually occurs. This might account for the descriptions you will hear from many paranormal researchers who have actually witnessed portals taking place where they state that they see partial manifestations that appear to consist of fog-like, mist, or even spectre type apparitions that may appear and then disappear. This may also account for the many sightings of what are known as shadow people, a very dark shadow shape of a person but no actual distinguishing features such as a face, clothing, etc, just the shape where we can tell their size, their build, or if possibly male, female, or even a child. A lot of times people witness what we tend to call ecto-plasma.

Ecto-Plasma in a funny sense is what we all witnessed slimed all over people in the classic movie *Ghostbusters*. We laughed at the time at this, but again Hollywood was drawing on their story concept from the real symbolism of what has actually been witnessed in this paranormal community over time as to evidence. Of course they were going overboard with it, but that was of course to garner laughs and humor. Ecto-Plasma has been witnessed by a select few people in this field and is rather hard to describe until you actually are able to witness it with your very own eyes. I myself have also witnessed it, but only on rare occasions and I have done a lot of investigations. I do know personally that what I witnessed with my own eyes was not of this world or dimension that we live in. I don't know exactly what I have seen, but it was coming from some place far and different from our own. Ecto-Plasm is believed to consist of a hypothetically form of bio-energy that is the actual energy interaction on two different dimensional planes that may enable ghostly materialization. It seems to be what is formed when a ghostly entity is able to form in our own dimensional environment. In other words, something coming through a possible portal and interacting with something here in our own dimensional plane of existence and the energy exchange is characterized as forming into this ecto-plasma substance.  It also is something that is very hard to capture on film for evidence purposes and there are some cases out there where it has been captured, but also a high degree of skepticism towards it.  I myself have shot great infra-red video straight at the ecto manifestation sources that I have witnessed with great focus, stabilization, and everything, and for whatever reason it would not appear on that film even though I could clearly see it with my eyes swirling around at the time.  This is usually the same story with other good paranormal researchers out there.  It is a strict game of chance to encounter and capture something like this on actual film where it is very clear.

I do tend to believe that with the concept of portals, we are getting closer and closer each and every day to truly understanding what they actually are.  I also believe that there will be more and more actual evidence captured that prove this theory that they do exist and are very real.  What portals are however, remains at this time to be a very large question in the minds of all serious paranormal researchers out there including myself, but very plausible solutions and hypothesis from people that really make sense are starting to flow in.

Another paranormal theory floating around out there amongst paranormal people about why ghosts may exist in our world is what is called the time-slip theory.  No, this theory does not mean that time literally trips and falls onto itself even though that does sound like a good way of looking at it.  Maybe it means that the clothing falls off at times in that it is totally naked, stripped, and put out there for all to see?  Who really knows, but there have been several well known people including Albert Einstein and the physicist Stephen Hawking who have come up with some possible explanations and theories about what time is, how it may exist, and how it may act around us.

Some scientists out there have even gone as far as to possibly say that they believe that time may exist in both past, present, and future in certain dimensions that interact or intersect with each other at the same times in different places. When I hear this, I do find it a very interesting and a clever concept. When I go outside, I sometimes just stand there and wonder if the reality of everything I see is actually there the way that I am seeing it, or is there something more there that may be unseen at any particular segment of time? Maybe what I am seeing is in effect purely an illusion? How do I know that what I am seeing with my eyes is truly there? We all pretty much accept that whatever our eyes and minds perceive around us as being all there really is, even though in reality, there is probably a whole lot more looking right at us at any given moment.

I know these sounds somewhat far-fetched, so let me elaborate a little more about how it is some of us in this research perceive ghosts to exist. When it comes to ghosts and interaction, we have several different types of experiences. I know this because I have listened to a lot of people over times who have witnessed ghostly encounters and their stories do have differences in them about how they see ghosts. We all hear the classic ghost stories, but some personal stories out there are rather interesting about what is being witnessed by people. A lot of people that witness ghosts describe them as not interacting at all, staring right through them, or acting out a certain scene that is played over and over again the same way each time. We refer to this as a residual haunting. It again is like a filmed scene being played out over time in the same manner and sometimes exactly the same time of day or night over and over again at different times of the year. Could this be related to the time theory from earlier? When we ask ourselves about residual hauntings, we also wonder what it is that causes this; does it have to do with a fluctuation of time such as a rift or slip?

When I think of time, I personally tend to think of time running in a fashion very similar to that of a computer program running. If there is a disturbance somewhere in the running of that program, then there will be some fluctuation to it such as a pause, complete stoppage, closing out of the program, sometimes a repeating action, etc. We know that with computers and when they run programs, that there is electricity running in it and current and that there are millions of processes taking place very fast as to given information being assimilated and calculated. Could time possibly also encounter the same effects at times due to outside influences? Could dimensional time as we know and experience it at periods possibly run up over itself or through itself at times? Time is also infinite as we know it. Do you feel that time in some way can be entrapped or do you not really look at time for what it is? People have encountered what are known as time slips and their versions and are strikingly different but in a lot of way very alike.

I have heard first hand accounts from people who were driving around, walking outside on the street, or even entering buildings when they all of a sudden encountered what is considered a ghostly time rift. A way of describing this is like a step back into the past or possibly even the past or future stepping into our time for a moment. I alone have witnessed many things ghostly and not of this world, but I have yet to encounter a time slip. I do hope for that moment I do actually witness this because I have heard from people that it simply is mind blowing and unbelievable when it does occur, that it really makes a person question the reality of what is right in front of our eyes.

Some of these stories as an example may consist of people walking into an ordinary older building and all of a sudden pass a room where they encounter a person either standing or sitting there in clothing that is not of this time. The person or persons usually do not interact at all or looking at people when

154

these time slip events occur. Sometimes, it may appear that they are looking at us, but maybe it is something instead maybe that they are hearing or seeing, that maybe they are seeing us standing there looking back at them and they cannot believe what it is they are seeing or hearing at the time. Someone was recently telling me their personal story on Facebook that they had entered a strange building just like this with another person and were walking down the hallway when they passed a room. They stopped and looked into the open doorway as they were walking to see a man sitting there in a smoking jacket with a pipe in his mouth reading a book. It was not necessarily this strange sight that got their attention, it was the fact that the whole room looked like something straight out of the 1930's. The whole décor of the room the way they described it looked like simply a big step back into time. They both immediately had stopped walking in this moment; they both stopped surprisingly to go back and look back into the open doorway only to discover then that the room looked entirely different than what they had seen before. It now looked like a modern office in modern times. They had both then exchanged to each other their versions of what had just happened and came to the conclusion that they had experienced and saw the exact same thing at that moment.

So, what exactly is considered a time slip? Most physicists will agree that time is one of the most perplexing and strangest unknown things in our known universe. There has been a lot of discussion about what time exactly is and how it may act around us. For the sake or boredom that extreme scientific discussion may cause, I will do my best to keep this idea simple here because otherwise I will lose all of you because some of this can be really really deep in this theory. What we do know of time is that there are indeed some people out there experiencing these things and we also know from our observations that these very rational minded educated people are not making these stories or accounts up. So, what is really happening here with this? We do also know from watching science fiction movies and from reading about this subject that the concept of time travel is not possible. Or is it.....yet? There have been pictures seen recently and analyzed that depict a picture of something from the past many years ago, and then you notice something else in the picture or film. You notice that there appears to be a person from the future on a cell phone or dressed in something modern standing or moving about in the picture or film, even though everyone else is wearing period dress. Some of this has now really gotten the media's attention on the internet in very thought provoking discussion and curiosity. If you would like to know if the idea of time travel may be possible or of time slips are real and occurring, then try to find someone who has actually encountered this and have them tell you their story. You will find their whole story very interesting, very thought provoking, but at the same time also very scary.

When I think of the time slip theory, I am going to go out on a ledge and share my thoughts about the concept of worm holes and the effects they may have on time to maybe cause these slips that are occurring. What's funny is that most of you have probably heard the concept of worm holes already from many great science fictions shows and movies that have been out there. Good examples of movies that have been out there portraying this concept are *The Philadelphia Experiment* or *The Final Countdown*. Again, a lot of the things that we hear from those shows or movies had to start from somewhere, and a lot of those terms and ideas were gathered and used from actual scientific books out there on the subject. Some of those concepts that we see may actually become a true reality one of these days as known technology increases and expands with new ideas and applications. I tend to think that the idea of the time slip theory is very plausible and having to do with some interaction of a worm hole possibly taking place at any particular place or time to cause that slip in time as we may perceive it.

When we think of wormholes, we think of it as being a shortcut through space or quite possibly even time. An easy way to think of what a wormhole is as to the concept is to pick up a piece of paper. Now draw the same size box on the top side of the paper and also draw a box on the bottom side of the paper. This is what we consider to be two dimensional in aspect on the paper. When we think of different universes being differently dimensional, we think of this piece of paper in exactly same way. This has always been a problem about known space travel from where we are to places very far out in space from us. This is because we do not have the necessary time, supplies, or fuel for an astronaut to travel those extreme distances to get to that other universe. This is where we consider the prospect of space that we see with our eyes and perceive with our minds possibly being something different than what we think it is. If we want to get from a point A in the first box we drew on the paper to a point B that is in the second box we drew, then the only way we would perceive this on the two dimensional paper would be to draw a straight long line intersecting one box to another. Time in same respect would also be taking place in us drawing this line. With the wormhole concept, what we do to shorten this and because another dimensional interaction, would be to fold the paper where we put one dimensional universe right on top of the other universe where they would possibly be interacting on the same dimensional plane with each other. In other words, a wormhole is punched through where space, time, and matter all travel through from one dimension to another. This is of course a very simple explanation of what a wormhole is, but it gives us a better understanding of what it is we are possibly working with here and thinking about. When time somehow enters a wormhole, what exactly is occurring with it? This might be the possible explanation to what a time slip is and why they occur sometimes.

Knowing what we know about time slip and ghosts, what would happen if we put a physicist and a ghost hunter together? Who knows? When we think of ghosts in this aspect as to a possible reason they may be appearing to us, it seems this could be some answer to the vast enigma we are encountering. It seems quite plausible that some ghosts that are seen or witnessed might be actually looping back and forth in a time slip through a wormhole. This a possibility and there are some people in this field including myself that are going even deeper with this concept in seeking some more answers through our research methods. We are not saying that this concept is the total reason that ghosts are appearing, we are saying that this may be a reason that some ghosts in certain non-interactive situations are witnessed the way that they are. We do this because there could even be a possibility that what we are seeing with our eyes may not exactly be what is out there in front of us at any given time or instance. In other words, don't just take for granted what you see or are led to believe is there. We need to open our minds even more to the possibilities.

Another popular paranormal theory floating around out there is called the concept of parallel universe. This is a clever concept and I tend to believe that this may be the case a lot of times when we are experiencing ghosts. When we think about this concept, we need to think about the fact that there may be different universe dimensions existing in the same place as our own even though we obviously cannot see or hear them. It is believed that the universe may have its own collective frequency by which it operates. Frequency change may very well be the key here. If our own universe that we live in every day is operating on a certain frequency that is constant and another universe is on another level, maybe there are fluctuations at times that cause different dimensions to coexist in the same time and space. This might be an example of why we see things; maybe they are seeing us also in these circumstances when these strange events occur. When we die and move on, maybe we are just continuing to another existence in another dimensional universe where physical matter is not needed. If frequency is the key, then we need to examine this further as to the resonances of the known universe. We do know that celestial stars in our universe seem too resonant at given frequencies, so this concept is very plausible.

When we think of this concept of parallel dimensional universes mixing with each other, it does make a lot of sense when we think about how EVP's are obtained and how we hear things that appear to come out of no where. It also explains when we get EVP's why they may also be asking a question as if they hear us or possibly don't see us. It may have to do with the universe and dimensions being like a huge tuning fork where any fluctuation may cause some dimensions to interact with each other. It is interesting when we think about this, because it appears to be a relatively simple possible theory to a concept that it so large.

I also I have possible paranormal theory of my own that I would like to share. I have always wondered from what I have seen and experienced why it is that many ghosts/spirits when witnessed appear sad looking or looking as if they are trying to give something or wanting us to find something. When you hear as many statements as I have over the years on what people see, I begin to wonder about this a lot. I tend to think that there is something more to all of this. I tend to think of a paranormal time elapse window existing.

When we die and pass on, maybe we are given the chance or opportunity to stick around to make sure that our loved ones are okay. Maybe we are allowed to look in on them just like in Charles Dickens story, to possibly change things if we can. I tend to believe that we are given something like a week in our time for this, sometimes we may be given longer. Maybe we are given as long as we like and that we can go back and forth if crisis arises for some reason. I do also tend to believe that there is a conduct rule on what a ghost/spirit can or cannot do while interacting with us. I also believe that some of them break this universal rule and maybe because of that, they are stuck here in a purgatory of sorts. Maybe this rule states that they are only allowed to show themselves to us at times for the better of things? Like getting a message to us personally or just letting us all know that they are still here. Maybe they are only allowed to do this a few times and if they do this more, then they break the rule and then have to answer to it? Maybe they are always in tune with us as to seeing or hearing us? That they are on the same frequency level and can witness everything just like we can?

We all know that we as human beings are given will power to make our own solitary choices whether those are good or bad choices. We also know that we as human beings make all sorts of daily mistakes in our lives. Some of us may consider ourselves good people until we are able to see in the mirror how we really are perceived by other people. Some of us live by very materialistic things while others live by fundamental deep values of good living and understanding. Some of us are very selfish while others are very giving. Maybe these are the things that we must learn to correct ourselves and maybe this is the reason why some loved ones choose to stick around so that we may see the light of understanding.

Just about every paranormal researcher has their own paranormal theories, some of them very alike while other somewhat different. Some are complex while others are very simple sounding. Some seem very plausible and understandable while others seem rather foreign, very hard to understand, and in the distance. What we do all know as paranormal researchers is that most of us do think alike. We are close or on the same page as to the ways that we all see the paranormal world. It is a big and strange world indeed and with a good sharing of knowledge we all get closer to understanding the mysteries that abound within this magical paranormal arena. If we continue to work on theories and share our knowledge with each other, then each day we move a step closer to having very solid answers as to what is actually occurring as to ghosts and why they may be here still.

# Chapter 10: Paranormal Experiments

I needed to have this chapter discussion in this book because any paranormal team that does not do any paranormal experimentation, well they really aren't a very good paranormal team. There is also always going to be a good every day discussion on this topic because of what is found out by doing different methods. Every paranormal team out there should be implementing experimentation into their investigations to find possible answers. Do not just walk around aimlessly in a dark environment every time trying to just see if there are any ghosts there.

Serious paranormal researchers in this field know that ghosts do exist and are a reality, so please take more steps in your investigations when you have the capabilities for something more. Go deeper and try to find how ghosts are able to do what they do and how they may be able to communicate with us. Find out better ways to communicate with them and help them to show themselves. The only way to do this is to be cleverly thinking all the time about experimentation methods to see if different results on evidence can be obtained. If you are a solid paranormal researcher in this field for the right reasons, then you are probably doing this already and that is very good. You are on the right track.

Now with paranormal experiments, there are different things that you as a paranormal researcher you can do to make your investigations more interesting. With video, try having a very controlled area set up with many EVP monitoring devices and motion detectors set up in an environment. Just take about six K2 meters and set them up in a circular grid pattern around this room controlled environment. Set up about two to four cameras, preferably two infra-red and two full spectrum cams at different angles around the room so that they do not affect each other's field of view. Now take one to two investigators sitting in this room environment conducting an EVP session and try to draw out something to interact with you. This is something I like to call "Setting up the Grid". By setting this correlative controlled grid pattern as to cameras and EMF devices, you as an investigator should be better able to gather stronger evidence if something does actually occur while you are conducting this experiment. If you want to go a step further, apply a green laser within the grid pattern to see if any actual movement is seen or can be captured.

A lot of the paranormal experiments utilized have to do with either communication or manifestation on video, or manipulation of devices like flashlights. There really are no direct paranormal experiments out there because everyone is doing something a little different, but the main thing to remember is that you want to try different things as to experimentation to see if you can get better correlative evidence results. A good paranormal researcher is a person who is always never satisfied and never stops. A good researcher is someone who is always on the go and constantly thinking of new ways to improve paranormal investigation results. For every new paranormal method or device that is introduced into the world of paranormal research, there is always going to be something even bigger and brighter for everyone over the horizon.

There are also some energy experiments that you can apply if you have the time and of course the money. One of these that I have used a little bit and do want to explore a little more is that of the plasma globe. I personally have always been intrigued with using these more during our investigations. I actually would love to have three of these placed in an equal triangle formation in an environment to see what occurs. We have all seen these static energy plasma globes in stores and some teams are going a little further with these. The idea behind these plasma globes is that any person touching the globe creates a fiery finger of light that reaches out and crashes against the side of the globe creating a spectacular effect and colorful images. The idea with these plasma globes is if a person can touch it and create that static energy effect, then why not a ghost touching it to show something invisible that might be there and interacting with the globe. If something like that is caught on camera and witnessed by different people, then it might possibly be used for paranormal evidence.

A lot of paranormal people out there will try to dismiss this and say that they have already done this with no results. Well, that is fine and may be true or it may not true, but we also do not know the degree of which they might have tried this experiment. Do not just take someone else's word that they tried something and that it did not work. I have seen too many people quickly try to discredit a paranormal idea once it is put out there. Some people become discouraged by this, and other people like me just keep trucking along with these ideas. The more personal ideas on paranormal experimentation that you come up to try, the better an investigator you will become in the end.

The idea that I have is to place a globe like this with two different video sources around it, both infra-red and full-spectrum. We do know that ghosts do utilize the environmental energy that might be present as well as our own bodily energy and of course our batteries, so why not think that a ghost might be attracted to a globe as well? This might possibly help them manifest to something more distinct and visible. There are also many different plasma type devices out there that consist of plasma globes, plasma columns, talking and singing plasma arcs, plasma fire disks, plasma tornado and ball lightning generators, plasma discs, and energy probes. You can easily see by looking up information on this why I find experimentation with these devices in the paranormal research field very interesting. There is so much more for us to learn as to the application of energy resources in our paranormal experimentation.

Another paranormal energy experimentation device is called the Van de Graaf Generator. There are simple and complex versions of this device, some small and some larger. This device is essentially an electrostatic generator source which utilizes a belt of some material like silk or some dielectric material running over a metal pulley system thus creating and accumulating very high electro-statically stable voltage charges. According to *Webster's Online Dictionary*, a dielectric is defined as any electrical insulator material where when placed in an electrical field, the electric charges do not flow directly through the material but rather shift from their positions creating a polarizing where positive and negative charges flow back and forth from pole to pole of the actual material. This creates an internal electric field. There is a hollow metal globe on the top of this device where the charge forms thus creating a strong energy field. It is believed by quite a few serious paranormal researchers that this device may somehow hold the key to being able to give ghosts/spirits more actual energy within an environment as to their manifestation.

This device, if used the right way and in the right experiment controlled measures, might possibly enable a full body apparition capability where this paranormal mystery might better be able to be filmed or documented.

Some of these larger energy devices can be rather costly and this is the reason that you do not see many teams experimenting with things like this. I do tend to go a lot deeper as to exploring the energy manifestation sources that ghosts/spirits use. There have been many occasions while I was out investigating with several paranormal devices and had also purchased several size and voltage batteries and most of my batteries if not all of them have become drained. I know from experiences such as this that ghosts are trying to draw on all the possible energy in an environment and it does appear that the more energy available, the better chances for them to communicate and appear to us. It is not known totally why the drainage of energy takes place, but it does happen quite frequently for paranormal teams out there and there has to be a strong unknown reason for it.

It also is the belief or idea that when a ghost/spirit manifests that there is some type of ionic variance in molecules or difference that causes electrical energy to be created. This is most likely very similar to how lightning is created when storms are created and move over the ground. I do tend to personally do a lot more experimentation in this area over time as I acquire more money and equipment. The one thing that many have found within this field and with paranormal experimentation is that it does take a lot of time, energy, and money to do this. A person cannot rush paranormal experimentation because that will not provide the true answers that are needed. Again, there are many paranormal experiments out there that can be tried by you or you can come up with some of your own. There is no right or wrong in paranormal experimentation. The results obtained usually show the true reality of what is out there. Good luck with your experiments in what you do and provide to this paranormal research world. Do not ever be afraid to share your findings and results with this world. Also, do not be put down by anyone making negative statements about your shown experiments or results. That will always occur. I could go on and on with this chapter because there are many paranormal ideas out there, but I will leave that for you to find out. All you have to do is take the personal initiative towards exploring all those great ideas.

# Chapter 11: Demonology and the Paranormal

I personally feel this is one of the most important chapters in this book and therefore this chapter is somewhat long as well. It is long for very important reasons. The paranormal research has just gone crazy when it comes to the demonic. I don't really know where this thinking comes from or where it started, but it is definitely out there and I see it every day from paranormal teams. What I see alarms myself and my wife Connie to a great degree. What we see is a lot of fear being unnecessarily put into the minds of people in this field. What we see are paranormal teams very quick to falsely label something just paranormal in nature being demonic. What we see are some paranormal television shows helping this along by characterizing paranormal entities being demonic when in fact they are not. What we see is this mass paranormal community hysteria that has been created by people falsely stating that things are demonic when in fact chances are high that they are not. Now, this is not to say that demonic forces are not at play in this world that we live, because they are real and very much are trying to destroy faith in people's minds and hearts as to God and the church.

Demonic forces are dangerous and are out there, but not in the ways that a lot of the paranormal community are depicting them to be. True demonic cases are very rare and far between when it comes to the paranormal field, but they do exist and are a dangerous reality for some. Most serious paranormal researchers like ourselves who have been doing this for several years and who have many paranormal case investigations under our belts, will state the definitive truth, that demonic cases are very rare and do not occur the way that most people would think they would.

When I talk about demonic cases, I talk from personal experience after having conducted paranormal case investigations and from the things that we have seen while doing those investigations. I also review what everyone else is stating out there on a daily basis as to this topic. There are some people out there that will characterize or label paranormal researchers as dabbling in demonic worship without understanding the field. This is a very serious stereotypical false perception that people like that out there have. This actually could not be any farther from the truth about who we are and what we do in the field. There are however paranormal teams out there making very drastic mistakes in how they do things and this stereotyping could be where some of this is coming from.

I have seen paranormal teams label everything they do as to being demonic on the evidence they found. I have seen paranormal teams state that something is demonic just on the fact that they felt it or that someone on the team got scratched or physically handled in some manner. What I ask when I see this is how some paranormal team can just simply label something demonic just on the basis of someone being scratched? Can't regular ghosts in a violent nature also scratch in the same manner? When we think of ghosts, we think of the way those people might have been while they were living. We also know that there are all sorts of people out there, nice people, mean people, selfish people, crazy people, and just purely sadistic evil people. Doesn't it seem logical to think that if some of these types of people were still around as ghosts, that they would be doing the exact same mannerisms in death as they were doing while living? If those people were violent while living, why wouldn't they still be violent in death as a ghost? All paranormal teams need to ask themselves these questions each and every time and have good deep discussion on what was found, and what evidence was acquired during those investigations.  Do not just jump the gun each and every time in stating that they have done demonic nature paranormal cases when in fact they have not.  I feel that some people out there claim this because they feel it catapults them over everyone else in this field.  That to me is a disturbing thought when people out there are doing this.  If someone out there is claiming that they encounter many demonic entities on nearly every paranormal case that they do, guess what, you then will not be considered very credible in this paranormal field.

There are also some religious people out there who will try to claim that by us going out as researchers and trying to investigate the paranormal, that we are actually doing evil and drawing out and attracting demonic and evil entities and that we are dabbling in devil worshipping.  The truth and reality of this in fact is that we are doing the exact opposite.  You see these things are already out there.  When we go out to investigate the paranormal, we are seeking the truths that are already existing out there, not drawing out or creating the evils.  I have always believed that with any good there will always be a balance with equal evil in this world.  I believe that it is the actions of people in the regular world and not the paranormal world that really draws out the evil side of things.  People conduct themselves a certain way each and every day that they wake up and live their lives.  People have choices that they must make in how they will act or if they will follow morals.  People also a lot of times do things that are not good......as in violent acts and negative ways such as physical and emotional abuse.

Guess what, all these people have will power and make those choices.  When I view the world especially with the news, all I tend to see these days are negative acts taking place all over.  I see people doing things wrong a lot of the time.  Now, when I encounter someone trying to state to me that I am doing something negative as to wanting to investigate the paranormal world of ghosts more and helping a lot of people sincerely and deeply with the paranormal when it can range from just simple paranormal activity to something very rare and dangerous as to demonic activity, then I actually feel that I am on a higher level as to goodness and faith in God than a lot of other people out there. The truth of the matter is that my wife and I are both Christians.

Demonic entities are again a true reality in the world that we live in, but they are also very rare. Many people watch Hollywood movies such as *The Exorcist*, *The Omen*, *The Exorcism of Emily Rose*, and think that this is how it is when it comes to demonic possession. The very true fact is that these movies are not the reality and are sensationalized a lot for the fun of watching and being scared. When most people think of demonic possession, they think of the spinning head, pea soup being vomited into the priest's face, or even someone crawling up on the wall like an insect. The truth is that I love to watch these types of movies because of the excitement I feel getting scared purely for entertainment value, but I also know from some experiences with this that there is a lot more out there as to demonic entities and a whole lot more for people to learn.

A lot of things that Hollywood has portrayed in these demonic possession movies is in fact some of the truths that are out there as to this. The churches will not readily admit it or make it a very open discussed topic, but demonic possession does exist for people out there. For those who are experiencing the real thing, it is very bad experience or a living hell so to speak for them. Demonic possession also a lot of times takes many years to show it self with someone. It is not just about all of a sudden something appearing and taking someone over. The reasons why some people are afflicted by true demonic possession are not yet known. There is no sure way of knowing how they are selected or preyed upon as to this. Perhaps it has something to do with how they live their lives or what dark and sinister things they do in their lives? With some of these cases, I have seen the use of Ouija boards and other dark objects. Could this be the reason that people were taking over, that they dabbled in something they should not have? Or perhaps it has something to do with their souls. Maybe they are pre-selected at birth as to this. Those very well could be some of the viable reasons.

I do know that there are many things I still have to learn as to demonology. My wife also has a very profound interest to read more books on this subject. Most people hear the name demonology and they automatically think that someone is doing something that they should not, that they are studying witchcraft, black magic, or something. Most of these books are on some back shelf in a bookstore not readily visible, but they are there being sold. There actually are a lot more of these types of books coming out now. The truth is that demonology is the study of the demons that are out there and what they do and how they may affect our lives. It is also a branch of theology. It is the study on what demons are, and how to deal with them. You see demons were never human to start with and thus do not have human characteristics that people may think. I do know that some people reading this are going to think that this guy is simply crazy because he is talking about demons. I will admit that I used to think I was crazy to want to explore this paranormal research world many years ago. I started off simple and acquired much knowledge along the way in any ways that I could. I again have done a lot of paranormal investigations over the years and I have witnessed a lot of people's paranormal cases firsthand. I still have a lot of paranormal knowledge to acquire as I get older because I intend to do this until the day that I die. My wife studies and researches this field by my side and she has the same curiosities that I possess when it comes to the paranormal and wanting to know more. Demonology is something that I only suggest for the really serious paranormal researchers out there to partake in. Also, I do wish that people in the paranormal field would quit calling everything paranormal they encounter a demon, it gets ridiculous after awhile.

When it comes to demonology and really grasping the concepts behind its foundations, a paranormal researcher can only learn through experience and the proper channels from people already in this field of the paranormal. We also are all constantly learning and I do not consider anyone to be an expert on this topic, but for some people to be more experienced than others as to it. I also know that something like this can be truly scary and frightening for anyone who goes deeper into it and I only suggest this field of research for the very serious paranormal researchers who have done their homework first. The only true way for a person to learn and witness is to actually be a part of some true rare demonic cases. True rare demonic cases only occur about 1% of the time, maybe less.

Before I go into what things a paranormal researcher should look for closely about knowing whether a case is a real demonic possession or not, I would like to describe a recent true demonic case that myself and my wife helped on along with the authority of the Catholic Church which involved a priest and a real exorcist. For purposes of strict privacy and confidentiality, I will not reveal in this book either the location or the names of the people who were affected by this particular demonic possession case. They know who they are and we know who they are and what they went through, we will just leave it at that. I am just going to draw upon what things both my wife and I, the Catholic priest, and others observed towards this case to give you an example. To show again how rare these true cases are, I have only done three true cases out of many paranormal cases that I believe involved something of a demonic entity nature in them as to demonic possession. This case I am going to describe here also took place and involved a Texas family.

When I first became aware of this female client and her family, I had received an email from her. In the paranormal world, this is usually how first contact is made with a potential client. They usually reply to you for help because they see your paranormal organization website. When I received her email, it was a plea for help and she stated that she had discussed with approximately two other paranormal teams who had done nothing to help her. She had contacted them, but all they did were email or phone calls to her discussing her case. Nothing more was done and she soon became frustrated because of what was happening to her, and the experiences were affecting her family and getting worse each and every day. She was in her twenties and this dark entity had been around since she was eight years old and had followed her from one location to the next over her life up until then, but now it was getting a lot worse in doing things to her and her family. She needed help with this, but she was not getting it from the paranormal teams she had contacted before talking about this with me.

When I first received this email from her, I must admit that I needed to know more because again I am always objective to any new case or people until I know all the facts. I had in the past received a lot of emails from people having to do with the paranormal and their questions, some were legit and others were way out there and appeared off their rocker. This email seemed innocent enough and I was really disturbed by the fact that she had contacted other paranormal team groups in the state of Texas before us and that they had done nothing in taking her seriously about what she was stating in her need for help with this. I decided that I would type out a list of questions in an email and send it to her to answer. This was a list of my objective assessment questions to get a better idea on what had been occurring in the past and also not in the present so that I could get a better idea on if this was real and how to approach it. This potential client also lived over a six hour drive one way, so I had to be sure she was serious if we were to take this trip later to help them with this. Again, we never have charged any clients for any services that we do, everything is entirely free from us including all our expenses that come out of our pockets as to gas, lodging, food, etc.

After I sent the questionnaire email, I then waited for a response. I figured it would take her a day to complete and return it back to me. Well, I waited a few days with nothing, and I did start to think that something was not real with it. On the third day of waiting, I finally did receive an email response back from her as to completion of most of the questions that I had put on there. She stated that she had received my questionnaire and was typing her answers when all of a sudden her computer went totally haywire and the page blanked out on her completely, and sometimes her computer would totally shut down on its own or power off for no apparent rational explanation. She said that this occurred when she was trying to communicate with me and that this type of thing had also occurred to her when she had contacted others trying to explain what was occurring to them, almost as if something unseen was controlling her computer and trying to block her communication with the outside world.

She stated that before contacting us, she had also contacted a Catholic priest who was experienced with this sort of thing and that she was also emailing and calling him for help with her case. She said that she had the same sort of communication problems while trying to talk with him about what was happening.

She said that her cell phone would cut out totally while in conversation with the priest. She said that this never happened when she was making calls to anyone else, only on those specific calls to the Catholic priest who was based out of New Mexico. She even said that her cell phone had started to do very strange things when calling her exact same phone number and leaving strange voicemail messages. One of the voicemail messages she had received seemed very unearthly and ominous sounding. She said that she would never actually hear her cell phone ring during the incoming call. That all of a sudden, the registered call would show up with her phone number being the actual location of where the phone call came from in the first place but was coming to the same cell phone. Then a day or so after this first occurred, the eerie voicemail message popped up when she said that she was talking to a friend of hers about all the strange things that had been happening to her and her strange cell phone occurrences. She said that when the voicemail message appeared, that really scared her.

I asked her to email me a copy of the ominous voicemail message so that I myself could listen to it. She did send it a few days later. When I heard it, it did sound really strange and there was a very strange voice on it. It sounded to me like the call coming from a very far away place and it was slightly distorted sounded and creepy sounding just like she had explained to me. I then called her and we discussed things a lot more. I could tell that she was very down to earth and sincere in her long story, and that it definitely was not made up. She had been plagued for twenty years by this very dark thing since she was only eight years old and that it appeared to definitely be following and trying to control her and her family.

She had described a dark shaped very tall man without any distinguishing features standing in her dark room one night when she was eight years old. She had never before ever seen anything like that or had paranormal experiences as a child, but that once he appeared and disappeared right afterwards, her whole life from that point forward became a literal nightmare of very strange paranormal things occurring. Each time she moved, it would die down again but start up a few months after moving to the new location. She felt that this thing was out to get her and was very afraid of it. I knew from everything that she had told me on the phone in our long discussions that she was being very honest with all of this and I could just feel the tension in her voice as she described all the paranormal things that had taken place in her life over the last 20 years. Her long list of extreme paranormal activity events over the years would make most people cringe.

I had initially told her that my wife and I did not have the financial resources at that time to make the seven hour road trip to their home. I told her then that it would be a month before we could get out there. I extremely regretted having to take that time due to the severity of their case, but sometimes these things occur to paranormal researchers that provide these limitations. It was about 10 days after this initial discussion with her that things really took a turn for the worse. I still to this day have a hard time understanding what exactly took place that night to make things so bad.

It was approximately 2:00 A.M. when my wife woke me up suddenly from a deep sleep that weekday telling me that my cell phone was just ringing over and over again. I had the phone on buzz mode so it was extremely annoying hearing it constantly buzzing. I answered the phone and found our female client on the phone in a desperate state. She stated that extreme paranormal events had been occurring to them the last four hours and had gotten worse and that her fiancé had become possessed by whatever it was, but he had just come out of it. She said that they did not know what to do and also called the Catholic priest who was assisting us on the case, and they had him on the other cell phone as well listening to the situation unfolding. I could hear how frantic everyone was on the other end of the line. She had a female friend staying with her as well and they were all encountering this event. I told her that I needed her to explain to me exactly what had occurred to them that night, so that I could help piece things together and make an assessment.

She stated that four hours earlier they were watching television in the living room and then started to hear some loud banging knocking noises coming from the back rooms down the hallway. There was no one down there at all and they stated this was a usual paranormal activity occurrence of the many that would occur at times, as if it was always trying to get their attention. This time she said the banging was very loud and disturbing and that her fiancé who was in Security Police in the Air Force and who had been previously stationed overseas in Afghanistan was extremely upset this time over what was happening. She stated that he stood in the hallway yelling out loud to whatever it was claiming that he wanted this thing to leave, that he was not afraid of it because he could tackle anything due to his military training, and that he could take this thing on personally. She said that he was yelling, confronting it, and telling it to leave his family alone. She said that both her and her friend were watching this happen for several minutes when all of a sudden he stopped all together and just stood there. He said that he had a really extreme headache starting to form and that he needed to lie down right away. It was at this moment she describes that the demonic possession event began to take control of him.

You see, she had always described this thing as following her from one location to another. When she had moved in with her fiancé about a year earlier, he had never once experienced anything paranormal in his life and was a bit skeptical even to the paranormal.

He did not necessarily believe in the paranormal, but he also did not readily believe in ghosts and haunting events as being reality. After he had laid down, she described how he kept holding his head and almost crying in pain as his headache become worse. She had gotten a cold watered down rag to give to him and none of this seemed to help. She then described how he closed his eyes and then did not say anything, and then started to breathe differently. She said that this occurred for about 10 minutes without him saying a word and then things really became strange.

She described that all of a sudden he had opened his eyes but that his eyes had a far distant non-emotional dark stare in them, almost as if his pupils had changed entirely. He lay still but then his breathing changed into very raspy breaths that somewhat animal like in their manner, almost as if he was growling every once in awhile. It was then that they had started the audio digital recorder and put it on the nightstand and just let it run while they tried to figure out what to do next. It was then that his voice and his mannerisms started to change. She said that he started to yell and chant very strange things, some of them understandable while other things not. He also yelled out to her that, "The priest cannot help you". He yelled this several times at her. She said that she had called the priest then and was talking to him about the situation and what to do. She said that he had heard on the phone what her fiancé was yelling and how his voice had changed like that of an animal. She said that she was extremely emotional and distraught at that time and felt helpless about what was occurring. She also was feeling that this whole thing was her fault. She said that it appeared the person that she loved and that she knew was all of a sudden was not there at all and that something else was.

I was on the phone with her for nearly 10 minutes when I remembered that she had previously mentioned that they had recorded this possession event. I was telling her that I wanted to hear that audio recording over the phone so that I could make my observations. She started the audio and I still to this day am shocked at what I heard on that recording. I heard a grown man change into something else. I heard what some will claim sounds like a demon. It was one of the most creepy, unnerving things that one can hear in this normal world that we all live in. It is one thing to hear something faked as in *The Exorcist*, it is another thing to hear something that is real. When one hears how a voice can change totally like that and say things that are very strange, it is downright scary. While I was collecting myself from being in shock while listening to the audio over the phone, it was then that her fiancé suddenly had the second demonic possession occur. During this event, both myself and my wife could clearly hear on speaker phone the whole thing and how extremely disturbing it was.

I could clearly see what she had been describing to me earlier because I could hear this grown man start to scream and moan wildly as if in a lot of pain and suffering. I could hear him tell them how much his head hurt and that he wanted it to go away. I then could also hear his voice change completely and heard him say some things in foreign language that sounded like Latin to me. I then asked for her to put the phone down towards him so that I could speak and I then read St. Michaels prayer out loud slowly word by word so that he could hear it. The moment I started to utter the prayer, he broke out in an extreme fit of anger, hate, and rage. Each word of the prayer only seemed to make him angrier.

This was not an animal that I was hearing on the other side of the phone, this sounded like a growling and spitting animal. I actually had to stop shortly after stating this because he was grabbing at them and they both were having a hard time keeping him restrained and laying down on the bed. She stated that it appeared that whatever was controlling his body was not strong enough yet to make the body sit or stand, and she was glad for that, but also afraid of what he could do to them at any minute as we carried forward. The Catholic priest also was on the other phone listening to all of this as well and offering his advice on how to carry forward. We eventually had both her and her friend read out loud St. Michael's prayer several times and what I will call for all purposes of what was heard and witnessed, the demon, left momentarily as suddenly as it had appeared. I could hear him all of a sudden come out of it and his breathing was very heavy and he stated that his throat was dry and hurt a lot, as if it had been on fire. While on the phone, they gave him several glasses of water and he had gotten up and gone outside. He also asked right away about what was going on and why was he lying in the bed and everyone looking at him. He had no recollection of that whole night except for when he was back in the hallway yelling at it.

That was all he could remember, and she said to me on the phone as well that he was still acting strange in his mannerisms and that she was now afraid of him about what he could do to her and the children. I told her then that there was not much we could do at that time due to the distance thing, even though I would have jumped right into my truck and drove if there had been financial resources to be able to do so. My wife Connie and I both had to calm her and her friend down and this took many minutes of reassurance that hopefully they would be okay for the rest of the night. We had been on the phone now for several minutes through this whole demonic possession event. My wife and I told her again that we would be in a lot of discussion and that we would both be there as fast as we could for further help on their case and situation. I remember hanging up the phone that night shaking after what I had heard and encountered. My wife and I talked about it for several minutes before we were able to go back to bed. We both knew then that we had to get there as fast as we were able to.

I was talking with our client for many days after that night and she had described to me that he still did not remember anything about that night but that no further events like that had occurred, but that paranormal things were still occurring in the house. They had an event occur right before that night where they had been watching television sitting on the couch one night and a heavy wax candle had lifted up on the other side of the room and was hurled with a lot of force right into the wall totally across the room in front of them. Nothing this extreme was happening now, but they were still hearing banging and knocking noises as well as movement throughout their house in the middle of the night. Things were still happening to them. I told her that it would be at least two weeks before we would be able to get there and they understood and were waiting patiently for our arrival. Our purpose was to go there to document what we could about their case, so this could all be provided to the Catholic Church authority for further review and guidance. My wife and I are Christian and not of the Catholic faith, but we will enlist the help of whomever we can when it comes to something like this. I had previously experienced things like this on some past cases, but nothing on this extreme level before. Our client had described one night in particular after that possession event that started to get me worried again.

She had stated that they had gone to bed and everyone fell asleep. She said that suddenly she was awakened to hearing a man's voice speaking out loud about something in the living room. She says that she was just lying there listening to it when it became clear to her that this was her fiancé's voice and it sounded like he was speaking to someone else in the other room behind the closed bedroom door. She also could not see any lights on, and wondered what this was and

183

that he had maybe gotten up as he sometimes did. But who the hell was he talking too? She could not make out what either of them were talking about. After a few minutes of listening to this, she suddenly turned over from her back to go back to sleep and realized that someone was sleeping next to her. She reached over and turned on the light, and lying beside her sound asleep was her fiancé. She said that she then got up out of bed and went and opened the bedroom door to look down the hallway into the living room area. She said that every light was off in the house and that there again was that distinct eerie uneasiness feeling as if something was there watching her from the other room. She said that was the worst feeling she had in a long time since the night of the possession event.

When my wife Connie and I were finally able to make the seven hour road trip to their house, we packed up all of our paranormal equipment in the truck and headed out. We were both not quite sure what to expect when we got there and we were both thinking of that night on the phone and what we had both heard with our own ears. We knew we were up against something evil and that we both had to be strong and stick to our guns on what we had set out to do. We also knew this was not going to be easy and that we had to be extremely careful because anything could happen to us or them when we got there and did our investigation for documentation purposes. We knew we had to rely on our faith to see us through the experience. When we finally did arrive and were finally able to meet them personally, we realized that they were both very down to earth honest people and again realized how much they needed our help. I had been previously in the Air Force myself as Security Police, so I had a lot in common with her fiancé and we talked a lot about the Air Force and other stuff in getting to know them better, before we set up for the actual paranormal investigation to take place. We determined that they were very sincere everyday people and that they also had a very big problem on their hands that they needed help solving. A lot of that discussion included how they felt about God and their relationship with God and how strong their faith was.

For the investigation, we set up and started it around 10 P.M. that night. I had set up a couple of video cameras on tripods at different angles, and we had a third video camera that was handheld to move around to document better as the session proceeded. We intended that night for documentation purposes to try to bring out what was possibly within him or in their house still. I intended to try to re-create the previous possession event so that this time we could both witness and record it, and then send the documentation for the Catholic Church Diocese to review. I had also had several conversations by phone with the Catholic priest who was involved and he had offered a lot of guidance and suggestions on doing this. He was also talking and consulting with the Archbishop as to gaining possible approval for a possible exorcism proceeding to take place in certain stages if it was shown and witnessed that something evil was indeed possessing and controlling her fiancé at the time.

Once we had everything set up, I decided that I wanted to film this session in the dark to better be able to see what may happen and to possibly increase the chances of something paranormal happening. They had one other male family member present as well. We had the other male family member sit on a chair behind myself and my wife and had the clients both sit together on a couch together. I then took our a Bible, and some other religious things including a special blessed medallion that a local priest had given the client about two weeks before when she had gone to see him as well. He had given this medallion to her and stated that it had been blessed by The Pope and would help to ward off any evil things. The client had given me this medallion as well to use. The only thing

185

that I did not have at that time was some holy water. The reason we did not have any holy water is because I had asked one of my paranormal team members to get this for us from a local church in our area and he said that he would, but he forgot to. I also had more special instruments that I was going to use as to a special test, my small extremely bright flashlight. I however did not mention to anyone that I had this flashlight and that I was going to use it for a special purpose if anything developed.

Once the video cameras were turned on and put on infrared mode, we turned off the lights and began. My wife Connie said a few prayers to begin for protection. I then instructed our clients that I was going to start a session to try to provoke and see if what had shown itself before, if it would show itself again. I started again with the reciting out loud and very clearly St. Michaels Prayer. I said it very slowly and with determination. The first two to three times I said it, nothing strange at all appeared. Both of the clients were still sitting on the couch watching myself and my wife. I then decided to have him recite line by line right after me the same prayer. The first time we did this, he seemed that he was okay to do it, but also somewhat reluctant as he recited right after me on each line. It appeared to me that each line seemed to be becoming harder and harder for him to say. It was during the second time that he reached up and stated that a very bad headache was beginning. He said that it really was beginning to throb in his head and was hurting quite a bit. He leaned forward at one point and put his head totally cupped in his hands on his lap and stayed that way for several minutes but was still reciting line by line after me. He then leaned back with his head on the couch and closed his eyes as if he was going to sleep.

My wife Connie had also told him before we began as to a sign to know that he was still here with us, this was a very quick two tap on the hand. Every

186

time we asked for the sign, he was supposed to do this. Up to now, he was doing this just fine every time we asked for it. At one point, he opened his eyes and looked straight at my wife and then at his partner, as if in a hate look. I asked him why he did that, but he did not really answer me, saying it was nothing. He then closed his eyes again while reciting line by line and suddenly stopped reciting all together. He just sat there and his breathing increased into heavy breaths. My wife immediately asked him for the sign and he just pushed her hands away. It was then that he opened his eyes and we saw that he was not there anymore, but someone or something else.

For reasons, at this point I am going to refer to the entity as "it" when I describe we believe we encountered that night. This thing did not feel or appear to ever have been human, due to its mannerisms, so this is the reason that I refer to it in this manner. It opened its eyes, cracked its neck a few times, and stared straight at me as if wondering who or what I was. I could feel inside a sudden change of atmosphere in the whole room, a very dreary heaviness of despair and tension, and environment where possibly we were not in control of anymore. It was something about his eyes and look, there was extreme hate and anger now in those eyes towards all of us in the room. It was like looking at a caged animal that wanted to get away. I then took my small very bright flashlight and without saying anything turned it on and flashed it into his eyes to see what would happen. You see, this flashlight is so bright that any human being reaction to it in the eyes will cause a person to involuntary blink and try to look away because it is too bright and hurts the eyes if shined in them. When I shined this flashlight into his eyes, he looked straight into the light, and did nothing, no blink, movement, or moisture in the eyes. Any normal person would have immediately teared up from this. I could also see that his pupils stayed the same and did not change according to the very bright light. Any normal person again would have had their pupils change due to the bright light. None of this was occurring. It was then that his voice changed totally as well, into that same creepy different sounding voice we heard on the phone weeks before. We knew that it had arrived.

Without going into extreme detail, we encountered two sessions where this thing threatened us several times. The first session lasted a few minutes and he came out of it as suddenly as he went into it and remembered nothing afterwards. He also claimed to be very thirsty upon coming out of it. During the second session, he went right back into it with a few prayers being said. It did not take as long this time around and it also seemed more powerful and angry this time around. I at one point took the blessed small medallion into my hand without telling it, and touched the back of his head with this hand. At that exact point where he could not have even felt the medallion in my hand, it went crazy and started to yell and curse at me. We continued to recite St. Michaels Prayer over and over again. It seemed to become more and more infuriated every time we said it, but at the same time it appeared to be becoming weaker. At one point, I put my silver crucifix also on his front forehead as well as the Bible on his head, demanding that it leave him. He grabbed my arm then and tried to stand up. I am a very big man at 6'-5" tall and very strong as well. I have to admit that when he grabbed my wrist, it felt like it was about to break from the pressure, that was how strong he was. While we were trying to hold him down, he suddenly passed out completely and went limp, slumping forward on the couch in a sitting position. He remained this way for several minutes before coming out of the possession and could not remember a thing again and as well drank what seemed like several bottles of water.

During the demonic possession, events that both my wife and I witnessed that night, I can clearly say that something not from this world had taken over his body and mind and was controlling him in very bad ways. The evil could easily be felt in the atmosphere of that room. We felt after bringing it forward, that it was definitely there and that more intervention and help was now needed from the Catholic Church so that an exorcism could be done and carried forward. The first step of the process of exorcism discussed and to be done by the Catholic priest was deliverance. He had gotten permission weeks later for this and proceeded to contact an exorcist to help out this couple with their holy problems.

We had done our part in all that we could as to documenting and trying to help this couple with what she had faced most of her life. You see, demonic possession is not for the light hearted or the amateur paranormal researchers out there. This is because many people can make serious mistakes if they try to take on something like this without the proper guidance, know how, and experience. There are certain signs to look for and document when it comes to a possible demonic possession being actually true: 1) extreme changes in personality, 2) sudden weight loss, 3) changes in sleep patterns, 4) extreme changes in attitudes, 5) self-mutilation, 6) a lot of swearing and cursing, 7) changes in personal hygiene, 8) destructive nature, 9) abusive or threatening violent nature, 10) sudden sexually open suggestive displays, 11) multiple personality changes, 11) occult items seen, 12) non-blinking of eyes, 13) catatonic states of stillness and staring, 14) changes in pupils as to darkening of the eyes, 15) Changes in facial features, different person, 16) Inhuman strength, 17) They may possess what is called 'retro-cognition' which is knowing of your past events they were not aware, 18) They may possess also 'precognition' which is ability to forecast future personal events, 19) They may know personal things about you even though you have never met before, 20) Changes in voice entirely, sometimes very animal like such as snorts, growling, etc., 21) They might read your thoughts, 22) They may move strangely as to how they walk, they may not actually walk but glide or float, 23) They may write or carve symbols into their skin on their body, 24) They might be able to levitate, 25) They might be able to move or levitate other objects, 26) They might totally change into what looks like another person, 27) Animals become very frightened of them, 28) They might be able to create very foul odors, and 28) They might be able to create paranormal activity such as scratching sounds, banging, or knocking noises on walls, ceiling, etc.

You can see from our experiences here that demonic possession is real and a very serious sinister problem within the paranormal world. The paranormal world can be very interesting and fun, but at the same time can be very dark and scary. There are things out there lurking beyond our imagination. You as a paranormal investigator in this field will also never really know when you are about to possibly encounter something from the dark side of this research field. It could happen at any time and you need to study and prepare yourself if that happens. Also, if you feel that you have encountered or witnessed something that you believe to be truly demonic in nature, please do the right thing and seek out qualified experienced help with it. You will only make the bad situation only better by doing that instead of being foolish and making a mistake. There again is much to learn from the field of demonology.

# Chapter 12: Ghostly Entities of the Paranormal

Okay, now that I wore you out with that last chapter on demonology....let's discuss other things a little brighter in the paranormal world. Before I do that, did you get your crucifix, holy water, bible, and wooden stakes all ready? You will need that! Just kidding, even though this paranormal world can be sinister and dark at times, it can also be very entertaining and enlightening as to what is discovered within it. It is hard to describe to someone new to this field how exciting that can really be without that person actually going out there and being subjected and witnessing the mysterious paranormal for themselves. Now that you have all of your protection devices are in your paranormal bag along with your equipment, let's move on to other things. There are different types of exciting ghostly entities and paranormal activity you might encounter while going out and exploring this field.

One of the most sought out so called prizes as to paranormal evidence in this field is the ability for a team to capture a clear full bodied apparition on video or by film. Paranormal teams out there all refer to this as being the holy grail of the paranormal evidence world. Nearly every paranormal team is working hard every day in trying to get this type of evidence. There are new video and camera filming devices entering this paranormal market every day, so I do feel that we are getting a lot closer as to this. I also feel that full spectrum capability is going to produce a lot more real and credible evidence. I do tend to think that infra-red capability is going to be a thing of the past in the next three to five years. There will be a shift phase towards everyone using full-spectrum in their investigations. It costs a lot of money to switch equipment, but in time most will see a full-spectrum camera on every paranormal team out there.

The next great thing about paranormal entities you might encounter are what are called shadow people. Shadow people are very exciting but also are very hard to capture on camera or video as good evidence. They are out there however, but again very hard to document. This is because they move very fast in the blink of an eye and seem to be very aware that we are trying to capture them on film and video. Shadow people have a very solid darkness outline to them against the darkness that is already there. You can see features of their outline pretty clearly, but you cannot see any facial or clothing features. You can always tell if it is a man, woman, boy, or girl though from the shape outline. Most shadow people as evidence are capture accidentally on either film or video. When you see an actual real shadow person, you will be talking about that experience for quite a long time because they are very interesting to witness.

Briefly, I am going to mention orbs and this is not because I like them or necessarily believe in them. Yes, there are true very real orbs out there in pictures and on film, but the real ones are very rare and the people who have gotten those have done their homework in proving that they are real. There are true deep characteristics to look for as to orbs. They must be giving off their own energy or light source against a background, they must be moving in strange patterns of travel as if they have a mind of their own, and they must not be dust, bugs, or an effect created by the camera or video camcorder in either regular film or infra-red. I will leave it at that as to orbs, because most of the pictures and videos of them that I see are not real and are naturally created. I get a lot of people constantly asking me to review their pictures or video as to orbs and for me to offer my honest opinion. I do offer my honest opinion as an investigator, but in a polite sincere professional objective viewpoint. I advise them that the picture or video is inconclusive as being any evidence of the paranormal, quite clear and concise. I don't believe in rambling on and on about a picture or video if there is nothing paranormal in it at all that I see. All I can say about orbs is that people need to look and review personally on what they have a lot closer and not waste time putting false and natural things out there. Debunk and analyze your own possible evidence is what I always say. If you are not doing this, then you are not being a serious paranormal investigator. You can tell from how I talk that orbs do not excite me.....I'd rather be mowing the lawn then discussing them in greater detail.

EVP's and ITC paranormal communication evidence to me are some of the most interesting things that we encounter in the paranormal. When you capture your first known and confirmed very clear EVP or ITC evidence, you will simply be jumping off your chair. It is just so amazing to hear something like this when you know there was no other possible reason it could have been created, except for the paranormal. To hear ghostly voices is one of the things that really drives my passion in this field. I find EVP direct communication to be something so close to actually speaking with a ghost. It shows that they are here and they are listening, especially, when you receive very direct loud clear answers to your personal questions. You will find that the ghosts are there and that they are willing to talk to you.

Cold spots or thermal temperature changes in an environment is also something of great interest and fascination to me as an investigator. When you stand in a very hot environment with a temperature of 90 degrees and you are totally sweating because there is no electricity in the building to run air conditioners, the building is very old and abandoned, all the air conditioners and power is turned off you will see what I mean when you encounter a paranormal cold spot. You will either move into a cold spot or it will move onto you suddenly and you will instantly feel very cold as if the temperature dropped several degrees for no apparent reason and no wind or anything like that. To describe it is like walking into a very cold deep freezer. You will usually also feel an electrical sensation when this same cold spot effect is felt. I have stood where the temperature was 90 degrees and very hot and where the temperature dropped 60 degrees and I could then see my breath coming out of my mouth. It usually does not last long when these paranormal occurrences happen to you, but those experiences are enough to keep you coming back for more, looking for a rational explanation. The problem with that and the paranormal is that there is no rational explanation for it.

The paranormal world is full of spectral and ghostly paranormal entities that you will encounter. You will at times possibly see apparitions, black mass shapes, shadow people, have feelings of being touched, possibly be scratched, grabbed, or thrown, hear footsteps or movement noises, hear banging or knocking noises, have things thrown at you. There are all things that could occur to you and more. You have to be ready to accept those things when they do occur to you. There can be very frightening when they occur because you are usually in a very dark environment when they do. As long as you are really prepared for what you may encounter while investigating things that go bump within this paranormal research field, then you have already made the first step towards it.

## Chapter 13: Paranormal Research Locations and Experiences

Yes, there is a chapter 13 in this book. And no, you will not be unlucky by reading it. As a paranormal investigator, I have had the opportunity to explore the paranormal world quite a lot and to investigate and see a lot of neat very haunted paranormal locations for myself. Over the years, I realized that my list has gotten a lot longer over time and I wanted to share with you some of the neat haunted paranormal research locations and experiences that I have had in those places. They personally were very interesting to see and experience. I still have a long list of unseen paranormal locations that I would like to get to one of these days. It takes time and money however to travel and investigate my long list of preferred haunted locations.

When people ask me, I always get one particular question asked all the time. People want to know what my favorite haunted paranormal location was. This is a very hard question for me to answer because I have seen some really neat haunted locations and I still have a lot more to see. I tend to really like the historical sites better than others and that is because of the old time feeling I get when investigating locations such as these. One of my favorite paranormal locations that I had the opportunity to investigate for myself was the Myrtles Plantation back in 2005.

The Haunted Myrtles Plantation, St. Francisville,
Louisiana 2005

Photo By Dan LaFave

Photo By Dan LaFave

I stayed there back in 2005 for 4 days and nights. I did this for a reason, and that was to stay in a different haunted room each and every night. I stayed in the General David Bradford suite, the Judge Clarke Woodruff Suite, the Fannie Williams room, and the William Winters room. What was very neat also about that whole stay there was that it was during the week when hardly anyone else was staying overnight at The Myrtles. I pretty much had run of the whole place for my own personal paranormal investigation. I have to admit that I did encounter a lot of paranormal things there that ranged from hearing voices and unseen people discussions, being touched, hearing loud footsteps, hearing what sounded like dishes and cups being clinked together as if a party or something was taking place, hearing music also playing at times. Walking around on that property at night just gives you the shivers because the whole place just takes on a very spooky atmosphere when you are alone and no one else around.

Photo By Dan LaFave

Photo By Dan LaFave

I also spotted what looked like apparitions walking around on the property at times as well as the clear apparition of what I believe to have been the slave servant Chloe standing by the fireplace  and window in our room in the Judge Clarke Woodruff Suite. I could see that she was wearing a head wrap on her head. I did not feel threatened by anything at the Myrtles during my visit, but I walked away from there with one of the best EVP's I have ever gotten......an EVP where three spirits (a woman, a girl, and an old man) all speaking at different times in a few seconds of each other on an audio recording. That very real EVP still amazes me to this day and is out there on Youtube for the world to listen to.

Photo By Dan LaFave

There was no doubt in my mind while walking the grounds of The Myrtles Plantation alone that I was being followed and watched. I had that feeling several times while I was there and especially at night when the plantation appeared to take on another look to it almost like a formation back to the 1700's when everything occurred there. At night, a person when alone does feel almost as if they are transported back to the era of plantation life.

St. Francisville, Louisiana Cemetery, Photo By Dan LaFave

The St. Francisville, Louisiana cemetery close to The Myrtles Plantation also was very old and spooky with a real gothic look and appeal to it. There were graves in that cemetery that I saw that went back several hundred years and crypts that were so old that they were in signs of decay. Just to walk around that cemetery close to dark was not an easy task for me; I could just feel the presence of many ghosts around me roaming at the time. Just to be in an old cemetery that old really was amazing to me. It was profound just to see something so old, historical, and still intact.

Photo By Dan LaFave

       Another haunted location that I have enjoyed immensely several times was Jefferson, Texas. The whole town and its cemetery has some type of haunted past to it as to stories and encounters. If you ever have the opportunity to visit this place for yourself and experience its ghosts, then you will see what I mean. There is the haunted Jefferson Hotel, Excelsior Hotel, The Pride House, the old haunted courthouse, The Grove, and many other haunted locations there as well. Stay in one of the hotels or bed and breakfasts for yourself to encounter the ghostly activity.

Front Side of Old Jefferson Hotel
Taken By Unknown Person – Not Subject To Copyright

Lobby of Jefferson Hotel
http://historicjeffersonhotel.com

There is a very good nightly ghost tour as well that you should take. The ghost tour will give you an idea of all the ghostly happenings in Jefferson. The neatest thing about Jefferson is that it is small, relatively hidden from the major highway, and you will feel as if you stepped back in time as you walk the old cobblestone streets.

Inside Old Wooden Stairwell, Jefferson Hotel
Photo By Dan LaFave

While in Jefferson, Texas please be sure to stop off at the very haunted "The Grove" which is owned by the author Mitchel Whitington and his wife. He has written several books on various things and the paranormal as to ghosts. They really are great people and I believe they may still offer a tour of their historic and very haunted home. There are too many ghost stories to cover here as to The Grove. If you are interested, just look up its story online and you will see plenty. I had the pleasure of meeting Mitchel and his wife several years ago. He did also personally autograph one of his books for me.

Picture By Dan LaFave
The Grove in Jefferson, Texas

Photo By Dan LaFave
Inside of The Grove

Another very good haunted paranormal location that I enjoyed exploring and had great experiences in was Presidio La Bahia which is located in Goliad, Texas. This is another haunted location that I have been to several times over the years and investigated the paranormal. You can rent the actual quarters overnight where the Mexican commanding officer would have stayed back in the days. You then have access to the whole garrison inner courtyard and towers.

Front Side of the Quarters Looking Towards the
Chapel
Photo By Dan LaFave


The Quarters used to be the actual officer
accommodations for the Mexican commanding officers
at Presidio La Bahia. Many very strange paranormal
encounters take place within The Quarters at night.
When alone in there, you really do get a strange
feeling and uneasiness.

Photo By Dan LaFave
The Old Mexican Officers Quarters,
(Where you can spend the night)

The backside of The Quarters opens up into one of the inner courtyards in front of the old chapel. There are some graves that are actually in this courtyard and some other unmarked graves all the way around the old chapel and along the wall. There also is an old well towards the back wall.

Photo By Dan LaFave
Front of Chapel within Presidio La Bahia

Picture by Dan LaFave
Taken from Inner Courtyard Presidio La Bahia

The inner back courtyard of the Presidio garrison is very large and was partially reconstructed and reconditioned in the 60's in a large project from what the compound originally looked like. The stone walls are very high around the whole garrison and an original cannon was found buried that now sits in one of the towers overlooking the outside.

Picture By Dan LaFave
Old Cannon at Presidio La Bahia

When a person walks up into one of these corner towers where the cannons are positioned, it is a distance of 20 to 30 feet to the ground outside which is quite a fall. Sitting in the towers at night is a neat feeling that takes a person back through time. On quiet misty nights up there, it is said and documented that people do hear and see ghostly things both outside and inside the garrison.

Picture By Dan LaFave

      The historical cemetery is right behind and to the right of the old Mexican garrison.  This garrison is the site of one of the bloodiest atrocities to ever affect Texas history.  On March 27, 1836, Colonel William Fannin and captive group of men were executed by orders of General Antonio Lopez de Santa Anna in what is called The Goliad Massacre.  This is the same Mexican general responsible for the attack on The Alamo in San Antonio.

      These Texas soldiers had been fighting for Texas independence from Mexico and had been captive in the Mexican garrison.  General Santa Anna, wanting to send out a fearsome dominance message to any other Texas soldiers willing to take a stand against him, ordered the men's slaughter to take place and for their bodies to be declothed and left on the ground exposed for the wild animals to eat on.  The bodies of all those men were left like that for nearly two months before being discovered later by Texas soldiers and they then were burned and buried in mass grave locations around the Presidio La Bahia garrison. During my paranormal investigations at night there, I have obtained quite a few very interesting EVP's. I also experienced some what looked like shadow people apparitions moving about quickly and then disappearing through stone walls. I have also heard very strange noises while walking the grounds of this large historical garrison at night. There is the story of a mysterious women and also an angry monk who have been seen walking the grounds. There are also accounts of the bell ringing late into the night.....even though the bell that is in the tower now is not real. It is just for looks. Many security guards in the past have reported witnessing and seeing soldiers on the grounds and hearing screams of pain and suffering.......those security guards quit soon after witnessing those paranormal events. The old stone Mexican garrison and the ghosts of those many Texas soldiers continue to tell their horrific stories of pain, suffering, and death. If you want to encounter a true very haunted historic place, stay overnight at the Presidio La Bahia and see for yourself.

I have many places that I again have seen, but one of the most haunted cities to witness for yourself if you get the chance is San Antonio, Texas. San Antonio is my birthplace, but I am not just telling you because of this, but that I consider San Antonio one of the most haunted cities in America. I have seen San Antonio shown on top ten haunted lists by several news sources. It has been ranked right up there with other famous haunted locations like Gettysburg, Pennsylvania, and New Orleans, Louisiana, and St. Augustine, Florida. I say this because I have had the opportunity to do paranormal investigations in several locations in San Antonio. There is the very haunted Victoria's Black Swan Inn, the Alamo, The Menger Hotel, The Crockett Hotel, The Alamodome, River

Center Mall, The San Antonio Missions, Grey Moss Inn, Fort Sam Houston, The Bullis House, The Alamo Street Restaurant and Theater, and many other countless other buildings. The list for this city as to haunted locations is very long compared to other cities.

Photo By Dan LaFave

Photo By Dan LaFave

Inside Main Room Parlor
Victoria's Black Swan Inn

This haunted atmosphere I believe is due to all the history that San Antonio shared in its foundations. Sure there are other haunted locations out there across the country, but if you really want to see some really good paranormal things, then come to San Antonio and see it for yourself. Texas in my opinion has a lot of ghosts and is a great state to live in and explore the paranormal world. I am always finding new and exciting paranormal places within Texas to explore and investigate. There again are many paranormal locations out there. If you are serious about this research field, please take the time to visit a lot of these places and witness the true beauty of ghosts.

# Chapter 14: Paranormal Television

We all love to watch paranormal television. Back in the days growing up, I used to love it when any television shows came on about the paranormal. There were great paranormal shows back in the 1970's like *In Search Of*. There however were not that many of them. The paranormal again was not even a word that was even known or used that much. No one knew what the meaning of the word was except for people that were researching this mysterious world of not talked about ghosts and hauntings behind the scenes and not on television. Paranormal television as a mainstream towards the television audience did not even come around until the paranormal show *Ghost Hunters* premiered on October 6, 2004 to the television world. I remember that day, because I had been investigating the paranormal world for several years already and wondered what this new paranormal investigation television world was about and what it would offer to the paranormal investigation world.

In all respect, the television show Ghost Hunters also started a fad sensation in a paranormal field that was already out there for many of us. It provided the fuel that was needed to really get the paranormal interest out there. We were already doing this the same way that they did it on television. So what was the big deal back then? I will tell you what the big deal was……..it had to do all of a sudden as to a big wide television group of various aged people suddenly realizing that ghosts and a possible haunted world were really out there. It had to do with all those personal haunted stories that we all have, that now possibly someone would really listen to those stories and provide some stories of their own. It involved a vast television world all of a sudden wanting to know and learn a whole lot more about paranormal investigation and ghosts. Watching these paranormal shows on television for many was the start of something very big, entertaining, and financially rewarding, the world of paranormal marketing as we say.

All in all, I have personally enjoyed the paranormal television world for what it is......entertainment value. What paranormal television has done in my thoughts is positively promoting the paranormal and bringing the reality of the paranormal world of ghosts and hauntings out there for many who would not otherwise have really known about it. It awakened a sleeping giant so to speak that was always out there. There also have been some bad circumstances that have occurred as a result of paranormal television.

One of the bad things that has happened in regards to paranormal television is that it appears that some things in high possibility and probability were faked on television for sensationalism and ratings. This in a lot of ways has hurt the credibility of the many serious paranormal researchers out there because now if some serious paranormal evidence is presented, it is severely scrutinized for possibly not being credible. It has made it that much harder for us to present our paranormal evidence to the world. That is okay, because all the serious paranormal researchers in this field will keep pushing on with our investigations whether or not the paranormal television shows keep coming or not. The saying is that we were doing this before paranormal television really got going about eight years ago and we will still be doing this if paranormal television dies out completely for now or goes through changes. I personally do believe that paranormal television is still strong and that it will continue on its trek as to garnering the amazement and curiosity of its viewers. I do also believe that older paranormal shows will eventually end and that new ones with new concepts will begin. I have heard from some that state that you cannot repeat or copycat the shows like *Ghost Hunters* and others who started the sensation.   My answer is clear and simple to this statement when I hear it.......you are right, we do not want to copy anything that is already out there as to the paranormal television world, what we now want to do is make it better than what paranormal shows that have already been or are still out there and ignite it with totally new paranormal television concepts.  No one ever wants to be considered or labeled a copy cat, I sure don't.

Myself, my wife, and our team, have had the great opportunity and luck to explore this paranormal television world for ourselves.   A lot of this is confidential so I cannot really say too much except to say that we have had the opportunity to film a paranormal pilot and present that to the major television networks to see if they would consider us for a paranormal television show.  We had the luck and opportunity to work with experienced New York based television producers on this concept and idea and hope for the best.  This is still in the works as I type these words.  I am not going to say anything else as to this except to say that it was fun and that we had an opportunity to see a lot of the ins and outs that go into putting together a large paranormal pilot project like this.   We had the opportunity to work with some outside people as well in a great paranormal haunted location and that we can truly state that the concept and idea that we have is totally different than what has already been out there in the paranormal television world.   We did not copycat one single thing and actually had about five totally different concepts going with this paranormal television pilot sizzle reel that was put together for the major television networks to review and decide upon.  We learned that television networks all look for something different, sometimes it is the characters, sometimes it is the story concept or idea.

As I write these words, we don't know what will happen with our pilot or chances, but we do know that we had fun in doing it and having the opportunity. We also felt grateful for the chance. In seeing a lot of what goes into projects behind the scenes like what we just did, I also have a realization of what occurs with many paranormal television shows out there. There are people out there who still state that they do like or do not like paranormal television shows for certain reasons. There are also others who state that they will not watch certain paranormal shows because of things that have occurred with them. We also know that some paranormal shows are more popular than others have been. We know that some original paranormal television shows have had many successful seasons while others only had one or two seasons before coming off the air for unknown reasons. We have also seen a lot of arguments, words exchanged, bad feelings, and bad attitudes within the paranormal television world. What we all need to do in this paranormal television world is to take it lighter heartedly and appreciate it more for what is there. Get rid of the bad attitudes, quit the argument as to who is better, have mutual respect for each other, and start enjoying paranormal television shows for what they really are and always have been.............pure entertainment. Now, go out there and enjoy it.

# Chapter 15: Paranormal Quest

In writing this book, it has been an extreme joy to put a lot of my thoughts into words for all who will have an interest in reading this book. This book is by far not perfect because the paranormal world, the world we live in, and all of us including me are not perfect by any means. We are constantly learning new things from each other and I listen and learn from a lot of you out there. I would also hope that you would listen and learn a lot from me. I am honest and up front when it comes to being a paranormal investigator. I speak from the heart when I share all of my personal paranormal experiences and guidance on how to properly investigate the paranormal world. I have met many people in this paranormal field and I hope to meet many more as I go on. Any people who have had the opportunity to personally meet me and talk about the paranormal research world realize that I like to talk about it and what I, my wife Connie, and our team do, learn, and what we have discovered. Those people who have had this opportunity to meet me usually either sit or stand around awhile discussing because we are all very down to earth people who like to talk about the paranormal. Maybe one of these days, you will have the opportunity to meet me at a paranormal book signing event or a paranormal conference.

I set out on a very long personal journey and quest several years back to find out more as to ghosts and the paranormal world. I saw and witnessed paranormal unknown things in the beginning that still to this day continue to intrigue me and draw me in to find out more. Yes, again this world can be scary at times due to things in it, but for the most part it is very enjoyable and informative. I learn new things each day because I am constantly looking for new information out there, whether that is from other paranormal researcher books or the internet as to articles. There is a constant flow of new paranormal information and evidence each new day. Some of it is good and some of it is bad, but at least the paranormal world community information is flowing for the purpose that it was put out there for in the first place, to inform the public world about ghosts. Ghosts again are real. Don't just take my word for that either just because I am saying it. Take what information that I have given you here in this book and go out there on your own personal quests if you are interested and see for yourself.

Paranormal haunted events when they occur will speak for themselves. All I ask is if you do choose to explore the world of ghosts and the paranormal more, just be sure that you do it in the right ways. I say this again because there are some people out there who are not doing it the right way or are possibly even exploiting this paranormal world for their own wrongful selfish financial means. There are not many people out there doing that, but people like this are there and are making a bad name for the rest of the other serious paranormal researchers like myself and others out there. I do not claim to be better than anyone else out there in this field. I do claim however to be very experienced and that I know what I, my wife Connie, and our team are doing as to the paranormal world. We strive in our life long quest in seeking the paranormal truth. We live by this in our lengthy quest. This again has been our motto from years back and will continue to be our motto that we follow as long as we do this, each and every day. I hope that I have enlightened you all to this very mysterious ghostly paranormal world some more and I hope that you gather and use some or all of my knowledge from the words in this book. This is my first paranormal research book and I do intend to write others, so stay tuned because I do intend to pass along more knowledge, information, and credible paranormal evidence as it becomes available to me. I am lucky because I have a loving and caring wife Connie who shares my same deep passion and interest as to wanting to investigate and explore ghosts and the paranormal. There are not many couples out there who share the same thoughts or ambitions and I find myself very fortunate to have her alongside me on our lifelong quest.

Now, enough talk........get out and go find some ghosts to talk to!!!!

# I Am I Said

I am I said
Others say who are you, are you dead
I am a person who the whole world a lot to share
Sadly other people out there don't seem to notice
or to care
I walk the endless roads of life with so much
knowledge to give
Maybe can make people better as they live
No one seems to want to listen or hear
If only they take time in their busy lives to lend a
real ear
So I continue to sit high and still on my
observation post
You see, I remain silent now from the past for the
moment
Because I am a ghost.


**Poem By Dan LaFave- Copyrighted**

Made in the USA
Charleston, SC
28 March 2012